The Freshwat

D0969621

Freshwater
FISHING TIPS

300 Tips for Catching More and Bigger Fish

Creative Publishing
international

Chanhassen, Minnesota

Creative Publishing
international

Copyright 2006
18705 Lake Drive East
Chanhassen, MN 55317
1-800-328-3895
www.creativepub.com

President/CEO: Ken Fund
Vice President/Publisher: Linda Ball
Vice President/Retail Sales & Marketing: Kevin Haas

Printing: R.R. Donnelley

10 9 8 7 6 5 4 3 2 1

FRESHWATER FISHING TIPS
   by Greg Breining, Dick Sternberg

Executive Editor, Outdoor Group: Barbara Harold
Creative Director: Brad Springer
Production Manager: Laura Hokkanen
Principal Photographer: William Lindner
Illustrator: Thomas Boll
Page Layout: Pamela Griffith
Cooperating Photographers: Kim Bailey, Doug Deutscher, Mike Hehner, Joann Kirk, Andy Lessin,
Mark Miller, Greg Ryan/Positive Reflections, Dick Sternberg, David Valdez/The White House

Cooperating Individuals and Agencies: Max Bachhuber; Keith Behn; Berkley, Inc. - John
Prochnow; Burger Brothers Sporting Goods; Delco Remy; Tom Dickson; Mark Emery; Fish
Lectonics - Mike Hunter; Butch Furtman; GNB, Incorporated - Dave Adams, John Miller; Dick
Grzywinski; Jim's Bait - Jim Keuten; Rod McGruder; Ed Metzgar; Minnesota Dept. of Natural
Resources - Don Schliep; Tom Neustrom; Tom Nightengale; Shakopee Marine - John Dobson;
Si-Tex Marine Electronics, Inc. - Roger Spencer; Stanley Spooner; Thorne Brothers - Greg Thorne,
Paul Thorne; Wayzata Bait & Tackle

Cooperating Manufacturers: Abu-Garcia, Inc.; Bass Pro Shops; Berkley, Inc./Trilene Fishing Line;
Bill Lewis Lures; Bill Norman Lures, Inc.; Blue Fox Tackle Corporation; Bomber Bait Company;
Brell Mar Products, Inc.; Cannon/S & K Products, Inc.; Classic Mfg./Culprit Lures; Daiwa
Corporation; Ditto Mfg., Inc.; Feldmann Eng. & Mfg. Co., Inc.; Fenwick; Fish World; Furuno USA,
Inc.; The Gaines Company; GNB, Incorporated; Hondex Marine Electronics; Johnson Fishing, Inc.;
K-M Products; Lindy-Little Joe, Inc.; G. Loomis, Inc.; Lowe Boats; Lowrance Electronics, Inc.; Lucky
Strike Mfg., Inc.; Lunker City; Mann's Bait Co.; Mercury Marine-Mariner Outboards; O. Mustad &
Son (USA), Inc.; Nordic Crestliner Boat Co.; Normark Corporation; Northland Fishing Tackle;
Plano Molding, Co.; Poe's; Pointmatic Corporation; Pradco; Producto Lure Co., Inc.; Rebel Lures;
St. Croix Rod Co.; A.C. Shiners, Inc.; Si-Tex Marine Electronics, Inc.; Slater's Jigs; Storm Mfg. Co.;
Stratos Boats, Inc.; Stren Fishing Line; Tru-Turn, Inc.; Uncle Josh Bait Company; Winter Fishing
Systems; Yamaha Motor Corp., USA

Library of Congress Cataloging-in-Publication Data

Freshwater fishing tips : 300 tips for catching more and bigger fish /by
the editors of Creative Publishing International.
                    p. cm.
   ISBN 1-58923-218-6 (soft cover)
   1. Fishing--Miscellanea. 2. Fishing--Equipment and supplies--Miscellanea.
I. Creative Publishing International. II. Title.
SH441.F786 2005
   799.1'1--dc22   2005002724

CONTENTS

CLEVER FISHING TIPS AND TRICKS HAVE PASSED FROM ANGLER TO ANGLER FOR AS LONG AS PEOPLE HAVE FISHED. The Greek philosopher Aristotle once wrote that a pair of fishermen could net the skate, a flat-bodied bottom fish, if one played music while the other danced on deck.

Most fishing tips, like Aristotle's, are of questionable value. Lots of the tips you find in books and magazines have not been thoroughly tested; they may have worked for somebody, but they don't work for you. Many so-called tips are common knowledge to anybody who spends much time on the water. Others are intended simply to sell you something.

What is a good tip? Certainly, it isn't a dissertation about how to find walleyes throughout the year. That's strategy. Nor is it a description of fishing dry flies for trout. That's a tactic. Strategy and tactics are the fundamentals of good angling, but they're too comprehensive to be called tips. And a good tip isn't a sales pitch for a high-priced, high-tech gizmo. That's not a tip, it's advertising.

Rather, a good tip is a specific solution to a vexing problem. The best ones are simple and cheap. They make your fishing easier or more enjoyable. A good tip will often trigger new ideas and help you fashion your own solutions. Most important of all, a good tip helps you catch more fish.

Our challenges in writing *Freshwater Fishing Tips* was to come up with little-known bits of information of real value to anglers. Gathering enough good tips to fill an entire book was a monumental task. We contacted thousands of the country's best guides and professional anglers. We tapped the memories of all the Hunting & Fishing Library staff members. During our travels, we fished with the best anglers in every part of the country. We watched closely to spot any unique twists in their fishing methods. We even solicited tips from celebrities and other famous fishermen.

After collecting thousands of tips, tricks and other morsels of advice, we sorted through them all, looking for those that were new, unusual, simple and, above all, helpful.

Then, the testing began. Our research staff spent hundreds of hours finding out if tips actually worked. If not, they experimented and tried to make the tip work. Many tips sounded good, but flopped when tested; these were eliminated. When we finished, we had more than 300 tips and tricks from North, South, East and West for nearly every species of fish that swims in fresh water. Where possible, we have given credit to the anglers who passed these tips our way (p. 190). Now we pass them on to you.

The tips are arranged into chapters. Some are general-purpose tips; others are best for certain species. Some tips show how to "doctor" lures to make them more effective. Others explain how to eliminate problems with rods, reels and other tackle. And you'll find tips on rigging your boat and trailer.

This is a book you'll want to read from cover to cover. Even if you're on the water every day, you're sure to discover something in this book that will improve your fishing. In fact, you'll find some of the tips so ingenious, you'll be tempted to say, "Why didn't I think of that?"

1

TIPS FROM FAMOUS
FISHERMEN

SNAG-RESISTANT WALLEYE JIG

Walleyes often hang out in snaggy cover where an ordinary jig would hang up almost immediately. You could use a jig with a weedguard to protect the hook, but many of these jigs are often fishless as well as snagless. Here's a rig that will allow you to work a lure over a snaggy bottom, yet there's no weedguard to reduce your hooking percentage:

MAKE a snag-resistant jig by pushing a 3- to 4-inch soft-plastic tube body over a floating jig head. Tie the jig head to a three-way swivel with an 8-inch length of monofilament. Attach a 1- to 2- foot dropper, slightly lighter than your main line, to the swivel; add a walking sinker. Tie the swivel to your main line, and tip the jig with a small minnow. Now the jig will ride well above bottom, and the walking sinker will slide over most snags. If you hang up, you lose only the sinker.

Al Lindner, Director of the In-Fisherman Communications Network, Brainerd, Minnesota

OUTSMART "EDUCATED" SALMON

You're fishing for Atlantic salmon and you get a rise, but the fish ignores the fly on subsequent casts. You change flies several times in an effort to attract the fish, but nothing works. Before you leave that fish, tie on the same fly that drew the rise. Often the salmon will strike immediately.

Lee Wulff, famous fly fisherman, fly tier and Atlantic salmon authority, Lew Beach, New York

DON'T OVERLOOK DOCKS

Fishing docks is a good strategy after a cold front passes. Bass that were holding around the edges of the dock before the front will tuck up into the thickest cover and deepest shade under the dock. Skip a plastic worm or jig as far back under the dock as possible, and retrieve very slowly. Also try fishing boat hoists next to docks; the underwater struts and posts provide security for inactive fish.

Guido Hibdon, 1989-90 BASS Angler of the Year, Gravois Mills, Missouri

BREAKING IN BUZZBAITS

Many bass anglers find that one buzzbait catches more than all their others – even those that seem identical. Chances are, the bait that works so well is old and beat up. The wear and tear on the prop pivot holes cause it to make more noise than a new lure, and that noise attracts bass. Here's a simple way to break in your new buzzbaits so they make as much noise and catch as many fish as the old ones do:

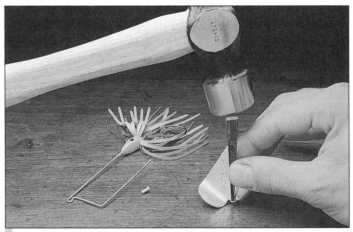

REMOVE the prop and drive the tip of a square masonry nail into the pivot holes to make them square. Reassemble the lure. The larger, square holes will make the blade rattle on the shaft.

Penny Berryman, winner of 1989 Missouri Invitational and other national tournaments, Dardanelle, Arkansas

CATCH THE BIGGEST MUSKIES

Casting bucktails and jerkbaits around shallow weedbeds and rock piles accounts for plenty of muskies, but not the biggest ones.

Muskies larger than 30 pounds spend most of their time in water deeper than 25 feet, assuming there is adequate forage at that depth. They're not likely to leave this zone to chase a lure skimming overhead, so you'll have to get the lure down to their level.

Troll slowly with a large, deep-diving plug, letting out line until you feel the lure hitting bottom regularly. Then, reel in a few feet so it hits just once in a while. Point the rod straight back as you troll. When a big fish hits, the line is straight from reel to plug, and the hook set is automatic.

Len Hartman, legendary big fish specialist credited with three muskies over 60 pounds, Ocala, Florida

EASY LINE-METERING METHOD

A troller needs to know how much line is trailing behind the boat. Here's an easy way to gauge the amount of line you let out:

COUNT the number of times the levelwind travels back and forth as you let out line. Try different amounts of line until you start catching fish. You can easily return to the productive depth by letting out the same number of passes.

Walter F. "Fritz" Mondale, vice president of the United States 1977-81, Minneapolis, Minnesota

PERSISTENCE PAYS

If at first you don't succeed, hang in there! If you're striking out, change lures and techniques until you find something that works. Keep your hook in the water and never give up.

George Bush, 41st president of the United States, 1989–93, Houston, Texas

USE THE SUN TO YOUR ADVANTAGE

When fishing the "flats" for bonefish, tarpon or permit, you must be able to see the fish so you know where to cast. If the sun is in your eyes, glare on the water makes it hard to spot your quarry. Keep the sun behind you and wear polarized sunglasses.

Stu Apte, holder of numerous saltwater world records, Islamoracla, Florida

2

GENERAL-PURPOSE
TIPS

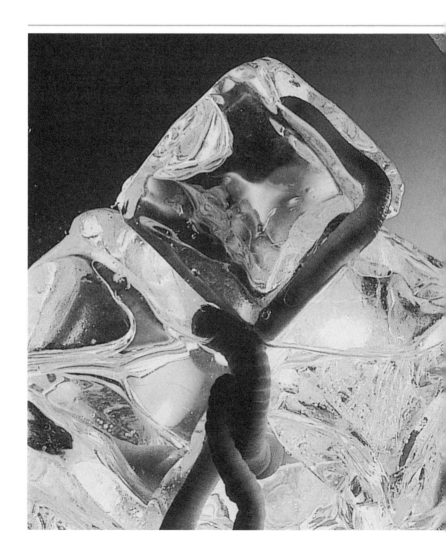

NO MORE MESSY WORMS

Digging through a pail full of worms and bedding makes a mess of your boat, hands and clothes. Instead, drop several dozen worms in a bucket of ice. Meltwater cleans the worms, and they'll survive all day. When you're done fishing, put the worms back into the bedding. If they crawl down, they're still healthy.

BRING THE WORMS TO YOU

To attract worms and keep them in a spot where they are easily gathered, make a worm bed. Place several inches of matted straw over dirt you have loosened and turned with a garden fork. Keep the straw moist to draw worms.

FISHING A WORM BENEATH A BOBBER

If you're fishing a nightcrawler with a slip-sinker, hook it once through the head so it trails behind the hook. But don't hook it this way when you bobber-fish because the worm will dangle vertically. You'll miss strikes, and fish will steal your bait. Here's a better way to hook your worm when bobber fishing:

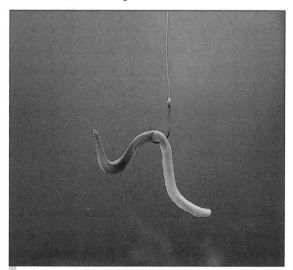

HOOK the worm twice through the middle when suspending it below a bobber. This way, you're more likely to hook a fish that doesn't suck in the entire worm.

LONG LIVE THE LEECHES

To ensure you always have leeches on hand, buy several pounds in the spring when they're plentiful and cheap. Leeches can be kept alive for months in a refrigerator. Take out only as many as you will need on your fishing trip. Most of the leeches you don't use will survive a day on the water and can be returned to the fridge. But keep them separate from leeches in long-term storage. Putting dead or dying leeches in with healthy ones may kill them all. Here's how to keep leeches in good shape:

STORE leeches in a Styrofoam bucket in a refrigerator; the water should be barely above freezing — 34 to 38°F. Change water every few days to keep it clean. Store an extra container of water in the refrigerator. When you change water, the fresh water will be at the same temperature and any chlorine will be gone.

ADD a few ice cubes to your bait bucket as you fish to keep the water cool. If the water is allowed to get warm, leeches begin to mature and spawn. The process begins at about 50° F and accelerates as the temperature rises. Once leeches mature, they die within several days, even if you return them to cold water.

KEEP CRAWLERS LIVELY

Worms kept in something other than a thick Styrofoam container get limp and lifeless on a warm day. If they get too hot, they'll die. Here's a way to keep worms lively, even in the hottest weather.

Put a few ice cubes in a small resealable plastic bag and bury it in the bedding. The worms will stay cool for hours. Without the bag, the melting ice cubes would make the bedding too soggy.

NIGHTCRAWLER SUBSTITUTE

If it's been too dry to collect nightcrawlers or if you can't find them at your local bait shop, it's tough to find a good substitute. Here's a trick that may salvage your fishing trip:

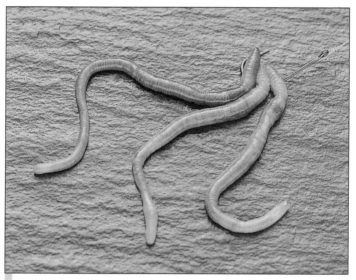

STRING three garden worms on a single hook. Push about 1/4 inch of the head of each worm onto the hook and let the tails wiggle freely. The squirming worms work as well as, and sometimes even better than, a crawler.

"EASY PICKINGS" FOR CRAWLERS

Because crawlers are so expensive, lots of anglers try to collect their own, but most are lucky to get enough for a day's fishing.

Here's how you can catch enough nightcrawlers in just an hour or two to last most of the season. All you need is an underground worm bed or an old refrigerator to keep them in.

• Most worm pickers go out at night, but you can often find more worms in early morning, especially if it has been drizzling all night. By morning, the worms are crawling some distance from their burrows, so catching them is easy. And you don't need a light. The best early-morning spots are golf course greens and the gutters along paved streets.

• Some golf courses produce lots of crawlers; others, very few. The trick is to find the ones that don't apply chemicals to control the worms.

• Check well-established lawns. A newly seeded or sodded lawn may not produce crawlers for several years, and if the soil is too sandy or gravelly, it may never produce.

• Look for crawlers during or after a prolonged light rain or drizzle. Worms don't like being pelted by heavy rain. The air temperature should be at least 50°F. Otherwise, worms stay in the ground.

• Wait until a couple of hours after dark so the night-crawlers are out of their burrows. If their tails are still anchored, the worms will zip back in when they detect a light or feel the vibrations from your footsteps.

• Cover your flashlight lens with red cellophane. This way, the light doesn't seem to bother the worms. Step lightly to keep vibrations to a minimum.

• Pick up crawlers on a paved street using a spatula. It's difficult to get your fingers under the wet, slippery worms.

FOLLOW BIRDS TO FISH

Birds can lead you to good ice-fishing spots. If there are no anglers or fish houses on a lake to give away the location of a hotspot, you can often pinpoint the site of recent fishing activity by watching birds, such as crows or gulls, which often congregate where anglers have discarded bait or small fish.

During the open-water season, look for loons, cormorants or fish-eating ducks diving in off-shore areas. The birds are feeding on small fish, which are probably relating to a reef or some kind of cover. Gamefish are likely to be there along with them.

ACCLIMATE MINNOWS

Most minnows are sensitive to rapid changes in water temperature. Always keep this in mind when handling your bait.

Many anglers believe they can keep their minnows alive on a hot day by adding ice. But they're often surprised to find all the minnows dead within minutes. Icing your minnows can help, but don't add too much ice at once. If you lower the temperature of the water by more than about 10°F at a time, the minnows will often die from temperature shock.

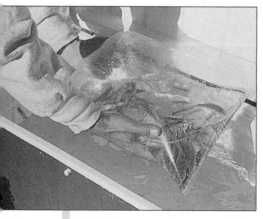

You can also kill minnows by moving them from cool water to warm. This problem occurs most frequently when anglers transfer minnows in a cool oxygen pack to the warm water of a cooler, bait well or flow-through minnow bucket. Solve the problem this way:

PLACE the unopened oxygen pack into a cooler or bait well to slowly warm the water inside the bag and acclimate the minnows to the change in temperature. After about a half-hour, the water in the pack will be the same temperature, and you can open the bag.

18

SEA ANCHOR SAVVY

Anglers on big water commonly use sea anchors to reduce their drifting or trolling speed. But sea anchors have many other boat-control applications. Here is one of them:

BACKTROLL with the wind by extending a sea anchor from your bow and running your motor in reverse. Without a sea anchor, the wind would swing your bow around, making precise boat control impossible. The sea anchor has enough drag to prevent the bow from switching around in the wind, so you can easily follow the bottom contour.

FINER FIDDLE FOR WORMS

Southeastern anglers collect grunt worms by "fiddling," rubbing an ax head or piece of steel on a wooden stake driven into the ground. The vibrations draw worms to the surface. Here's a way to make a stake that produces stronger vibrations with less effort and will help you get more worms.

Cut 1/4-inch-deep saw kerfs at 1/2-inch intervals along one side of a 2 x 2 stake about 30 inches long. Make a point on one end and drive the stake about a foot into the ground.

Rub another stick, such as a piece of broom handle, rapidly up and down across the saw cuts.

SAVE BUG DOPE FOR BUGS

If you get insect repellent containing DEET on your hands, it can soften vinyl fly line coatings, weaken monofilament line, damage lure finishes, eat away at line spools, dissolve non-wormproof tackle boxes and damage the screens of liquid crystal recorders. Here's a way to avoid the problem:

Apply the bug dope first to the backs of your hands. Then use the backs of your hands to spread the repellent to your face, neck and arms. This is a good tip for the camp cook as well, so the repellent doesn't get in the food.

PREVENT LINE TWIST

When you're jigging vertically, whether in open water or through the ice, the lure usually spins around and causes severe line twist. The twisted line tends to wrap around your rod tip and tangle in your guides. To prevent the problem, tie a small swivel to your line, a foot or two above the lure.

AVOID BOBBER STOP HANG-UPS

The advantage of a slip-bobber over a regular bobber is that you can cast it easily, even when you're fishing deep. But the bobber stop can interfere with casting. If it happens to wind onto the front edge of your spool, it can catch outgoing line, causing your cast to fall short or to stop suddenly and snap off the bait. Here's how to avoid the problem:

Reach down with your index or middle finger as the bobber stop reaches the bail and guide the line toward the rear of the spool. Then continue reeling as you normally would. With the bobber stop out the way, the line will peel smoothly off the spool on the cast and won't hang up.

UNWRAP LINE QUICKLY

It's happened to nearly every angler: when you're fishing, you notice a wrap of line around your rod. You're not sure how the wrap got there, but it seems the only way to get rid of it is to restring your rod. Here's an easier way:

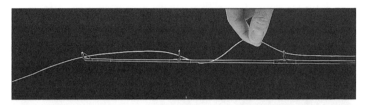
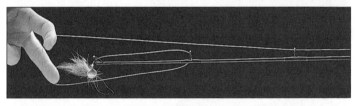
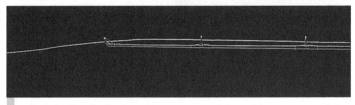

GRAB the line (top) where it wraps around the rod between two of the guides. PULL the line over the tiptop or butt of the rod (middle), which-ever is easier. RELEASE the line (bottom), and the line runs from guide to guide without the once-around wrap.

TRIGGER STRIKES WHILE TROLLING

When you're trolling with plugs, spinners or spoons, drop your rod tip back once in a while rather than maintain a steady pull. Dropping back causes the lure to tumble momentarily, triggering strikes from any fish that may be following.

HEADING OFF A BIRD'S NEST

If you're using a spinning reel and retrieve without much tension on the line, a loop of mono will often form at the front of the spool and interfere with the outgoing line as you cast. If you try to peel off line to get rid of the loop, the loop will also begin to peel off and tangle with the other line, often forming a snarl several feet long. It may be impossible to untangle the line without cutting it.

Here's a good way to head off a tangle before it occurs and save precious fishing time:

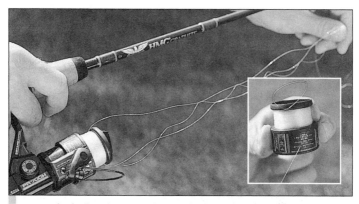

OPEN the bail and remove the spool when you notice that a loop has formed. Because these loops form at the front of the spool, it's best to pull line off the back of the spool to avoid tangling the outgoing line with the loop. After you pull off the loop, replace the spool, close the bail and reel in the loose line.

CUT A BACKLASH SHORT

Even expert baitcasters get backlashes, especially when they're casting into the wind. Here's a trick that minimizes the amount of line involved in a bird's nest and keeps you from ruining all the line on your spool:

LAY a piece of plastic tape across the spool after stripping out a bit more line than you're likely to cast. Reel the line over the tape. Now, even if you get a backlash, the tangle will go no deeper than the tape. If you have to cut the line to clear the spool, you'll still have plenty left.

BOBBER HELPS YOU GET UNSNAGGED

River rats know that if you snag your lure downstream, you may be able to pull free by letting out enough line to form a belly several yards below the snag. When you give a sharp tug, water resistance against the line produces a downstream pull that may free the lure. But if the lure is tightly snagged, this technique won't work. Here's a way to produce a stronger downstream pull and free the lure:

WIND

CLIP a big bobber to the eye of a snap-swivel. Close the snap over your line. Open your bail and let the current carry the bobber well past the snag. Close your bail. When the line tightens, give a sharp tug. The added resistance of the bobber results in a stronger downstream pull than that produced by the line alone. Other floats, such as a plastic bottles, will also work, and these can be partially filled with water to increase the drag and the power of your pull.

BONUS FOR PADDLERS

Trolling in deep, open water may seem like a waste of time, but some anglers who canoe the wilderness lakes of the northern states and Canada know differently. When paddling across open expanses, they toss out a lure, such as a crankbait or minnow plug. Pike, walleyes, lake trout and smallmouth bass often suspend in open water, feeding on ciscoes, a common baitfish in many of these lakes. Trolling across the middle of a lake is not a high-percentage method, but it produces a surprising number of fish.

DIAGNOSE FLY-CASTING FAULTS

A good forward cast is easy for most fly fishermen because they can watch the fly line and correct their casting faults. The problem is the backcast: It's tough to glance backwards over your shoulder to make adjustments to your casting stroke. For that reason, many fishermen have lousy backcasts and cast poorly overall.

If you have trouble with your backcast, such as hitting the water or ground behind you with the line, use this trick to study your problem and correct it:

(1) STAND sideways to your target (a Hula Hoop makes a good one) with your feet spread comfortably, like a batter standing at the plate. Lower your rod so it is parallel to the ground and cast sidearm rather than overhand. (2) WATCH the fly line as you make your backcast and forward cast. Adjust your timing and casting stroke until the line unfurls smoothly, forming narrow loops forward and backward. (3) TURN back toward your target and cast with an overhand motion instead of sidearm. The timing and motion remain nearly identical, even though the casting plane changes from horizontal to vertical.

SMOOTH FLY CASTING FROM A BOAT

When fly fishing from a boat, anglers usually drop extra line in loose coils near their feet. On the cast, the line will lift up and zip through the guides – unless you happen to be standing on it. Cutting a cast short this way is especially frustrating when fishing for shallow-water trophies such as tarpon or bonefish.

Your chances are few, so quick, accurate casts are essential. You can eliminate the problem by fishing without shoes so you can feel any line underfoot. Be sure the area is free of hooks, and if it's sunny, remember to apply sunblock to protect the tops of your feet from a bad burn.

TRY TAILWATERS AFTER HEAVY RAINS

Heavy rains cause most streams to rise quickly and turn muddy. The dirty water usually ruins fishing, but you may be able to salvage your trip by moving to the tailwaters of a good-sized reservoir. Silt settles out in the reservoir, so even after a torrential rain, water flowing from the dam will be relatively clear for some distance downstream. It will stay clear until it is muddied by tributaries.

FLY-FISHING IN THE WIND

Wind gives fly fishermen fits. You can't drive your forward cast into the wind. And a wind at your back causes the backcast to pile up, which means the forward cast is no good either. But wind doesn't have to ruin your fly fishing. Here's how to make good casts, either into the wind or with it:

CASTING INTO THE WIND. Cast sidearm, keeping your forward cast as low to the water as possible. This way, the wind has little effect on it. Loft your backcast a bit so the wind helps straighten it out.

MORE ACCURATE SPINNING

One problem with open-face spinning: it isn't as accurate at short distances as baitcasting. The baitcaster can lightly thumb the spool to control the cast or press down to stop the plug and make it land in just the right spot.

But once an angler casts a spinning outfit, it's tough to stop the lure on target – unless you use this trick.

Slide your hand back on the handle far enough so you can pinch the line against the spool with your index finger. Flip the bail and cast, releasing line by moving your finger. You can slow the lure down by feathering the line with your index finger, or press the spool to end the cast. This trick works only with small and medium-sized reels; big reels are mounted too far off the rod to reach with your finger.

AVOID A GUMMY MESS

Soft-plastic lures will react with many other items in your tackle box, bonding the materials together and bleeding the colors. The warmer the weather, the faster the reaction takes place.

All soft-plastic lures are made of polyvinyl chloride, the same plastic that makes up a rigid PVC pipe. The lures are softer than the pipe because they contain more petroleum-based "plasticizer." The plasticizer oozes to the surface of the lure and dissolves such things as plastic hook boxes, tackle boxes that aren't "worm-proof," paint on many lures, and "living rubber" spinnerbait skirts and jig dressings.

Take plastic grubs off spinnerbaits at the end of the day. Sort all soft plastics by color and store them in separate worm-proof compartments or in plastic bags.

CASTING WITH THE WIND. Cast sidearm, keeping your backcast low and shorter than normal. Aim higher with the forward cast so the wind will catch it, adding to your distance.

FIGHT FISH SMART

If you hook a large, powerful fish with normal-weight tackle, you may not be able to wear it down by lifting with steady tension. The fish can resist without moving much and doesn't get tired. Here are a couple ways to tire big fish quickly and increase your odds of landing them.

Work a fish in shallow water by pulling it to one side, switching the rod to the other side and pulling from the opposite direction. Pulling from the side with the rod tip low to the water forces the fish to struggle to regain its balance, so it tires quickly. The closer the fish is, the more effectively you can use the rod to wear it down.

If a large fish is sulking underneath the boat, work it with short, quick pumps of the rod, taking in just a few inches of line each time. Those quick tugs get a fish off the bottom and moving in your direction better than either a steady pull or a long, slow pumping motion.

EXTEND "CASTING" DISTANCE

Success in pier or shore fishing means getting your bait to the fish. If they're too far out, you can't cast to them. Here's a way to use an offshore breeze to get your bait to those hard-to-reach fish:

DOUBLE up your line about a foot above your baited hook and thread the loop (left) through a Lifesaver candy. PASS the loop over the Lifesaver so it cinches up against the candy (center) and keeps it from sliding on the line. Blow up a balloon and tie a knot in the stem. TIE the balloon to the Lifesaver (right) with a few inches of line.

DROP the rig in the water and let the offshore wind carry the balloon out. After about 15 minutes (less if you suck on the candy first), the Lifesaver will dissolve and drop the bait to the bottom.

EASY-TO-SEE ICE-FISHING LINE

The light, clear monofilament used when ice fishing for panfish is difficult to see. You can't tell when your lure is on the bottom, and you can't see the line on the ice. Solve the problem by spooling up with 4-pound-test fluorescent yellow monofilament, which is easy to see. Use a 3-foot leader of clear mono, which is nearly invisible to the fish.

NO-TANGLE THROW ROPE

A long rope can save the life of someone who has fallen overboard and is struggling in the water. But it takes too long to untangle a rope that lies in a heap in the bottom of the boat.

Here's a system of rigging a long throw rope so it can be thrown immediately and accurately. It's handy not only in boating accidents, but in ice-fishing mishaps as well.

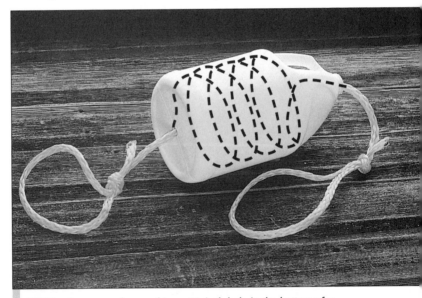

MAKE a throw rope by punching a ³/8-inch hole in the bottom of a plastic jug. Thread 50 feet of ³/8-inch rope through the bottom hole and out the top. Tie a loop at each end. Pull one knot snug against the outside bottom of the jug. Feed the rest of the rope into the mouth of the bottle.

DE-ICING YOUR AUGER

After cutting a hole in the ice, most fishermen set their auger down in the snow: But snow sticks to the wet blades, turns to slush and freezes solid within minutes. Once frozen, the ice is difficult to get off, and if too much builds up on the blades and threads of the auger, the tool won't cut. Here's a simple way to keep your hand or power auger ice free:

KNOCK the ice off the auger with a small hammer you carry in your ice-fishing gear. Be careful not to nick the cutting edge with the hammer.

TOSS the rope to a victim by holding the loop at the mouth of the jug, grabbing the jug by the handle and throwing it underhand. The rope will peel out smoothly from the mouth as the jug sails through the air. The victim can get a firm hold of the loop at the jug end.

HANDY MINNOW STORAGE

Ice fishermen often end the day with a good supply of healthy minnows. Rather than carry them home or throw them away, you can keep them beneath the ice at your fish house. Here's how to store them so they stay healthy for days and are easy to retrieve on your next trip:

POUR the minnows (top) into a perforated can attached to a 6-foot rope with a stick tied to the other end. Lower the can down a hole drilled just outside the house, as close as possible to the fishing hole inside the house. Let the rope freeze into the ice. RETRIEVE the minnows (bottom) by sliding a long hook made from a coat hanger down your ice-fishing hole. Snag the cord, hoist the can into the fish house, and pour the minnows into your bait bucket. When you're done for the day, sink the minnows back down the fishing hole.

ICE-FISHING SAFETY

Unfortunately, some of the year's best ice fishing occurs when the ice is most dangerous: right after freeze-up and just before ice-out. Unless you're sure the ice is safe, stay off it, no matter how well the fish are biting.

River ice can be especially treacherous. The current weakens it and keeps it from freezing uniformly.

Anytime you're ice fishing early or late in the season or on a river, take extra precautions. Test the ice thickness with a sharp ice chisel, and carry an ice pick so you can pull yourself out if you do fall through. Here are a couple of other tips for crossing ice safely.

Carry a long stick or sapling. If you fall in, the stick will bridge the hole and provide support so you can lift yourself onto solid ice. If a friend falls through, you can crawl over the ice, pushing the stick in front of you to reach him and help pull him to safety.

Wear a life vest under your coat. If you break through, the vest will keep you afloat and conserve body heat. A good alternative is a "float coat," which looks like a regular parka but has built-in flotation.

Fishing With Kids

Fishing can provide a lifetime of enjoyment for your kids, if you get them started right. If you don't, they'll sour on fishing at a young age.

Taking a kid fishing can be fun for both of you if you go about it properly. Here are some tips that can make the experience more enjoyable.

Do whatever seems most fun to the child. Be flexible. Most kids love to bobber-fish. It's fun seeing the bobber go under. If the kid wants to cast big plugs for sunfish, that's okay. It may not be the best way to catch them, but your kid will have fun casting and may just hook a big fish of some other kind.

Pick an interesting spot to do your fishing, someplace where there are lots of things to see other than water. Try fishing a small lake where you can make periodic trips to shore to break up the day. Or, try float-fishing a stream. You're always on the move, and there are plenty of sandbars and riffles to explore along the way.

Bank fishing gives your kids plenty of room to roam if they lose interest in fishing.

The middle of a big lake is the worst place to go, even if the fishing is terrific. Kids will soon tire of fishing and won't find much else to keep them interested. Soon, they'll want to go home.

Give your kids plenty of help when it's needed, but don't overdo it. If possible, let them bait their own hook, cast, and reel in the fish. If you do everything, you'll turn them into bored onlookers.

Don't force your children to go with you if they don't want to. Keep the trip short, and don't make them stay when they've run out of patience. You may be able to maintain their interest by bringing along a surprise, such as a toy, book, game or candy bar. Keep the treat secret and pull it out when they're starting to get bored. But when their interest has clearly waned, head for home. If you make them stay too long, they won't want to go along next time.

Be patient. Don't bawl kids out for tangling the line, spilling the tackle box or losing a fish. Make up your mind that this trip is primarily for the kids' enjoyment. You'll surely have to devote a lot of time to untangling lines and cleaning up messes, so if you want to do some serious fishing, leave your kids at home.

COMFORT IS IMPORTANT

Be sure children are warm, well fed and protected from bugs and sun. They have a much lower tolerance for sun and cold than adults do. Take along extra jackets even though it seems warm outside, and remember to bring their sunglasses. Don't force children to go with you in bad weather; you don't want them to associate fishing with being miserable. Be prepared to make frequent bathroom stops.

OUTFIT your kid with a comfortable life vest. Kids may not want to wear a bulky Mae West-type life jacket because it is awkward to fish in and not very stylish.

SIMPLEST IS BEST

Keep the fishing simple. Too often we expect kids to enjoy fishing that's way over their heads. No matter how well the fish are biting, you'll have a tough time selling a 7-year-old on fly fishing or backtrolling live-bait rigs. These methods demand too much patience and practice. As your kids grow older and get more interested in the sport, treat them more like adults.

USE simple tackle. One of the easiest outfits to use – and one of the hardest to break – is a cheap cane or extension pole rigged with a bobber and live bait. Also good are push-button spincast outfits. Spinning and baitcasting gear tangles too easily, frustrating both of you.

ANY FISH IS A PRIZE

Fast action is more important than big fish. By kid standards, a dozen sunnies are better than one 5-pound bass. Your job is to get them into plenty of hungry, gullible fish. Brag up anything your kid catches. Remember that a fish doesn't have to be a prize by your standards. Any fish is a trophy if you say it is.

Try fishing panfish, especially around spawning time, when the fish are concentrated in shallow water and eager to take live bait or small lures. Or, go to a lake stuffed with bullheads. Another good option is white bass fishing, particularly when the bass are chasing baitfish on the surface. They hit hard, and you can often catch one on every cast.

GAMEFISH
TIPS

Largemouth & Smallmouth Bass Tips

BETTER "PEGGING" TECHNIQUE

Plastic-worm anglers peg bullet sinkers with toothpicks to keep the worm and sinker from separating on the cast and retrieve. But the toothpicks jam in the holes, making the sinkers difficult to remove and later reuse without first punching out the toothpick. Here's a method that lets you re-rig quickly:

SLIP a rubber sinker stop onto your line before adding the bullet sinker, hook and worm. To re-rig, simply slide the stop up the line a few inches, snip off the hook, change sinkers, tie on a new hook and slide the stop back into place.

MONO LOOP FENDS OFF WEEDS

Texas-rigged worms are weedless, but with the hook buried in the worm, you'll miss fish. A worm hooked on a plain jig head has an exposed hook, so you'll hook more fish but snag more weeds. Here's how to rig a worm so it's nearly weedless but still allows a good hook set:

(1) TIE a piece of 30-pound stiff mono behind the eye of a 1/0 straight-shank worm hook. Run the line through the eye. (2) SLIDE the worm on the hook, and poke the mono into the worm at the hook bend so the mono forms a loop over the hook point. The loop is stiff enough to fend off weeds and brush but supple enough to give on a strike. Fish the worm with a bullet sinker. Set the hook as soon as a bass hits.

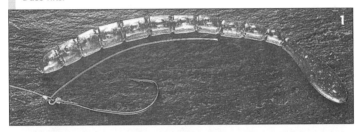

PLASTIC SURGERY IMPROVES WORMS

If bass ignore a normal plastic worm, try a high-buoyancy worm made with air bubbles in the plastic, such as a Sportsman's Super Floater, and enhance its action with a razor blade or X-Acto knife.

Slice the worm lengthwise, from the midpoint to the tail. Then slice each half lengthwise again to form four tentacles. Thread the worm on a jig. With the jig head on the bottom, the tentacles wiggle enticingly.

KEEP CURLY-TAILS FROM TWISTING

If you're bothered by severe line twist after casting with a curly-tail plastic worm, you're not alone. Even if the worm is hooked straight, without a kink in the body, it may twist on the retrieve. Here's how to rig a curly-tail worm to keep it from spinning and twisting your line:

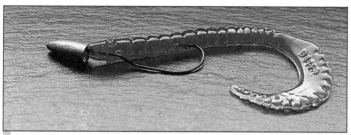

HOOK the worm so the curly-tail rides down when the hook point rides up. Make sure the body isn't kinked. If the tail's turned up, the worm is much more likely to spin as it moves through the water.

WIND IN RUSHES TRIGGERS BASS

When a strong wind begins whipping a bed of bulrushes, largemouth bass will move from the cover inside the bed to the windward points, where they ambush prey and smash lures for two to three hours. Then the bass quit feeding and return to heavy cover or move deep.

FAST REEL HELPS IN SLOP

A high-speed reel gives you a big advantage when bass fishing in slop. First, you can get your lure back to the boat in a hurry so you can clean off weeds.

Second, a high-speed reel helps you get a better hook set. You need to hold the rod tip high to keep your lure out of the vegetation, but then you have little hook-setting power. The high gear ratio makes it possible to drop the rod tip, rapidly take up slack, then set the hook.

Third, a high-speed reel enables you to quickly lift a fish and keep it from diving into the slop.

STIFF ROD RIPS WEEDS

A rod with good backbone works best for ripping a crankbait through weeds. You can't get enough snap with a soft rod to tear the weeds, so they stay on the lure. But with a stiff rod, you can rip the lure free with one sharp tug.

SECRET HUMPS

River fishermen know that smallmouth bass and walleyes hold behind bridge pilings to get out of the current, so most of these spots are heavily fished. But there's another kind of cover associated with bridges that is harder to spot and is fished less often. As bridge builders sank bridge footings, they would excavate boulders and rubble from the riverbed and dump the material in a pile nearby. Use your depth finder to sound the riverbed in the vicinity of the bridge to find these submerged rock piles. Most anglers overlook such spots, yet they make ideal cover for smallmouth, walleyes and other gamefish.

FLOATING LINE HELPS WALK THE DOG

"Walking the dog" – working a stickbait so it dodges side to side across a surface – is a proven technique for bass. Give the bait a sharp twitch and give it a bit of slack as it veers to one side. When the bait stops, twitch it again and give it slack as it glides in the other direction. Continue the retrieve so the plug dodges side to side as you bring it toward the boat. It's a great way to raise bass out of sub-merged weeds, brush or timber.

But you'll run into a problem if you let the bait lie motionless for several seconds. The monofilament will sink and the bait will nose-dive rather than dart to the side. Here's how you can solve the problem:

RUB a candle or fly floatant over the first 6 feet of line up from the lure. Either substance will float the line.

BANG JIGS FOR BASS

If you're over a school of bass on a rock pile, but ordinary jigging fails to trigger them to strike, get their attention by "banging" a jig.

Drop a heavy jig to the bottom, raise it up a few inches and let it fall. Continue to bounce it on the rocks with short vertical movements of the rod. It's hard for bass to ignore the repeated clunking.

KEEP PORK RIND FRESH

Left in the open air and hot sun, pork rind quickly dries and loses its suppleness and action. When you set down a pork rind lure for a while but don't want to return the pork to the jar, wrap the pork in a damp rag. When you unwrap the pork later in the day, it will still be soft and full of action.

WRITE OFF WEEDS

Spinnerbaits are a favorite for bass in heavy cover. They're nearly weedless, but the swivel often catches bits of fine weed, stopping the blade. Here's a way to use a ballpoint pen to keep the swivel weed free:

CUT the last ³/₄ inch to 1 inch off the pointed top of a ballpoint pen (top). Poke or drill a small hole through the tip. Using a needlenose pliers, open up the loop at the end of the spinner arm and remove the swivel and spinner blade. SLIDE the plastic cone onto the spinner arm (bottom). Then reattach the blade and push the cone back along the arm so it covers the swivel.

PACK PORK IN PLASTIC BAGS

Jars of pork rind are bulky. To carry pork in a vest or small tackle box, pack a few pieces and some of the brine in a small resealable plastic bag.

ADD SPICE TO SPINNERBAITS

Many anglers fish shiners for bass, but when the bait dies, they simply throw it away. Instead, you can use the shiner to tip a skirtless spinnerbait. It makes the lure more attractive and also slows the sink rate so you can work near the surface without speeding up the retrieve. Here's how to rig the minnow:

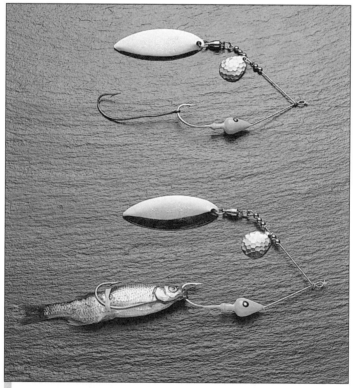

SLIP a worm hook (top) with an offset shank onto the spinnerbait hook as a trailer. HOOK the shiner through the lips (bottom) with the spinnerbait hook, and bind it to the trailer with a rubber band. The offset shank lets the hook lie flat against the minnow.

WEEDGUARDS FOR LIGHT COVER

In sparse weeds or brush, nylon-bristle weedguards may protect the hook more than is necessary, causing missed strikes. Here's a simple way to modify the weedguard:

CLIP several bristles at the base with a scissors or nail clipper. A dozen or so fibers remaining (bottom) will protect the hook in thin cover and yet be supple enough to hook most of the fish that hit.

EASY-TO-OPEN PORK RIND

As you use pork rind, the brine corrodes the cover of the jar and forms a salty deposit on the threads. As a result, the jar can be impossible to open by hand. Try this trick to keep the cover from sticking.

Spread a thin coat of petroleum jelly on the threads of the cover and jar when you first use the pork rind; repeat occasionally during the season. The petroleum jelly will prevent corrosion and lubricate the cover, so it comes off easily.

WEEDGUARDS FOR HEAVY COVER

In slop, thick lily pads, bulrushes or timber, ordinary weedless jigs still hang up because the nylon bristles don't shield the hook point from the sides. A quick adjustment makes the weedguards work better.

Flare the bristles across the point and heat them with a lighter or match. Be careful not to melt them. The nylon will take a set and stay in position.

VERTICAL JIGGING FROM A DISTANCE

Jigging directly below the boat catches bass in cold weather or at other times when fish are inactive. It's hard for a bass to resist the temptation of a jig repeatedly bouncing right in front of its nose. But if the water is clear, you can't park your boat directly over fish without spooking them. Try this instead:

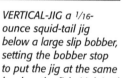

VERTICAL-JIG a ¹/₁₆-ounce squid-tail jig below a large slip bobber, setting the bobber stop to put the jig at the same level as the fish (right). The large bobber has enough flotation and water resistance (left) so a sharp pull will lift the jig rather than sink the bobber or pull it back toward you.

SAVE LIGHT TIPPETS

Fly fishermen who stalk small, clear streams for smallmouth bass often find that light tippets used with tiny jigs and poppers are a winning combination. But the continual shock of false-casting even these small lures will eventually weaken a clinch knot tied with a 4-pound-test tippet. If you don't retie often, you may lose a big fish.

Solve the problem by using a Duncan loop instead of a clinch knot or other knot that snubs down on the hook. The Duncan loop better withstands the shock of false casting a weighted fly. As a bonus, the loop allows small poppers and jigs freer play for better action.

PREVENT LINE TWIST WITH BASS BUGS

Large bass bugs, especially frog imitations with big splayed legs, may spin in the air as you cast, twisting your leader and line. Attaching the lure to a snap-swivel will eliminate line twist but will also cause a bug to ride low in the water or sink, ruining the action. Here's a way to keep twist out of your line without sinking the bug:

ATTACH a short piece of 30-pound mono to the fly line. Tie the mono to a small swivel; attach the leader to the other end of the swivel. The swivel may sink the tip of the fly line, but it won't affect the bug.

GOOD VIBRATIONS

Fishing gets tough with a sudden change in weather – the dreaded cold front. Still, cold-front bass aren't impossible to catch. Bass are sure to notice big baits that make strong vibrations in the water. Here are a couple of examples.

A big, single-bladed spinnerbait with a size 6 or 8 Colorado blade produces a strong, slow vibration that can tempt lethargic bass. Put a jumbo pork frog on the hook to slow the sink rate. Cast the lure into heavy cover and retrieve slowly.

Crankbaits run deep enough to reach bass that have been pushed into deeper water by a cold front, and the strong vibrations can trigger strikes, even from inactive bass. Cast out a big, sinking, deep-diving crankbait. Reel fast to get it deep, then slow down so it swims along the bottom.

LOOKING FOR ACTIVE FISH

Under cold-front conditions, most anglers slow down their presentation to entice fish that aren't interested in feeding. Some fishermen, however, do just the opposite: they work fast, hoping to find and catch the few fish that are relatively active.

Fish water you know well and move quickly from one proven spot to another, fishing each no more than 10 minutes. Pepper the areas with lures you can work fast, such as spinnerbaits and crankbaits. By covering a lot of water, you should be able to find a few active, catchable bass.

"DOODLIN'" BRASS AND GLASS

Doodlin' – twitching a Texas-rigged plastic worm along the bottom – catches bass in a lot of situations, but it can be one of the best approaches to try after a cold front has passed. Doodlin' can be even more effective if you add a brass bullet weight and a glass bead to the worm. As you're trolling, drifting or retrieving, twitch the rod tip rapidly, keeping the worm on the bottom. The brass and glass will click together, making far more noise than an ordinary lead sinker. Here's how to rig the brass and glass:

SLIDE a brass bullet weight and a good-sized glass bead onto 6-pound-test monofilament. Tie on a worm hook and rig a plastic worm Texas style. Brass is not as dense as lead, so you'll need a larger-than-normal sinker to get down.

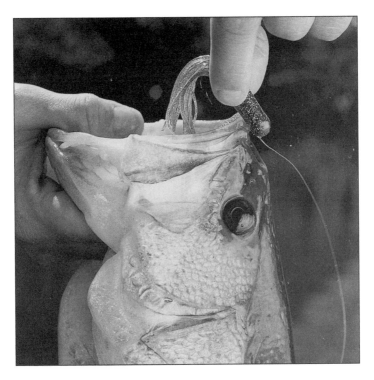

SLOW AND SUBTLE

Although big, noisy lures can catch cold-front bass, a slow presentation with a small lure usually works better. Here's one proven method for cold-front bass: Rig up with clear, light mono and a 1/16-ounce to 1/8-ounce tube jig. If the water is deep or cloudy enough that you can put the boat over fish without spooking them, try vertical jigging, which lets you work a lure right in front of fish until one decides to strike.

If the water is clear or shallow, and scaring fish is a possibility, cast and jig instead. Either way, work the jig as slowly as you can.

FINDING WEEDLINE BASS

As a cold front passes, bass holding at various depths along a weedline move to the base of the weeds. Inside turns in the weedline are usually best.

JIGGING A WORM IN PLACE

Working a Texas-rigged plastic worm slowly through heavy cover is an effective cold-front technique. But even the slowest retrieve may be too fast when bass are off the bite. Here's a way to entice them.

When the worm hangs up on submerged branches or weeds, resist your first reaction to rip it free. Instead, after you feel the sinker hit the obstruction, drop the rod tip a bit so the worm sinks a few inches. Then pull the line tight again to raise the worm. If a bass is around, the action of a worm jigged repeatedly in front of its nose may be too much to resist.

TARGET SHALLOW WEEDS

With the change in weather, many bass will head to the thickest weeds available. Some of this cover may be deep, some as shallow as 3 or 4 feet. Make best use of your time by trying the shallow weeds first.

In the shallows you can easily see where the cover is thickest and provides the most security, so you can flip or pitch a jig-and-pig or plastic worm practically on a fish's nose. Getting close in deeper water is far more difficult, because you can't see the nooks and crannies of the cover and aren't so sure where fish are likely to be holding.

STICK TO BREAD-AND-BUTTER SPOTS

Fish the spots that normally produce bass; exploring new water is a bad bet when fish aren't feeding. Usually bass will be in the areas you found them before the front passed. But they may hold tighter to cover or in slightly deeper water.

Walleye & Sauger Tips

A ROCKY START FOR WALLEYES

Look for early-season walleyes on rock piles in water less than 10 feet deep. The rocks absorb sunlight and warm the surrounding water. Most of the lake is still cold, so walleyes are attracted to these zones of warmer water. These areas appeal to walleyes for another reason: The warmth activates invertebrates, which attract baitfish on which the walleyes feed. Walleyes frequent big boulders later in the year as well. The large rocks cast shadows where the walleyes can hide and avoid bright sunlight.

GO LIGHT AFTER A COLD FRONT

Walleyes and saugers don't feed much following a cold front. But they may nip at a small, slow-moving bait. Here's a trick that can put a few walleyes in your boat when fishing really gets tough.

Spool a light spinning outfit with 2- to 4-pound mono, tie on a 1/16- or 1/32-ounce jig and tip it with a small minnow or leech. Use a trolling motor to keep your boat over a spot where you suspect fish are holding, then drop the jig to bottom. Lift and lower it slowly, move it in very short hops or just hold it steady; set the hook if you feel a tap or the line tightens. One problem: light jigs are tough to fish in windy weather.

DOUBLE BAIT FOR BIG FISH

If you're catching only little walleyes and saugers, you may be using minnows that are too small. Bigger fish often want bigger bait. If you run out of big minnows, here's a way to save the day:

HOOK two small minnows on a jig or split-shot rig. Don't bury the hook too deeply or the minnows will jam up in the bend of the hook and won't trail naturally.

JIGS FOR WEED WALLEYES

Stocked walleyes spend a lot of time in the thick vegetation usually associated with largemouth bass. You can catch these walleyes by casting jigs into this heavy cover. But ordinary walleye jigs don't work well; the exposed hook point and attachment eye on top of the jig head snag weeds. And most weedless bass jigs are too big.

Try a 1/8-ounce weedless jig with the attachment eye at the front of the head, which lets the lure slip through weeds easily. Some of these jigs also have a flattened head to slow the sink rate, so you can swim them over very dense weeds.

CHECK THE DOWNWIND SIDE

On a windy day, walleye anglers normally fish the wind-ward side of an underwater hump or point. But there are also times when fish feed on the downwind side. On a shallow hump or point, strong wind whips up a great deal of turbulence, causing various kinds of invertebrates to drift off the downwind side of the rocks. Baitfish gather to feed on the small organisms. Then gamefish, including walleyes, largemouth bass and muskies, move in to feed on the baitfish.

A LONG REACH MEANS FEWER SNAGS

Submerged boulder piles and rocky reefs are top spots for walleyes. But it's nearly impossible to fish a jig or slip-sinker rig in the rocks without getting hung up. You can minimize snags by keeping your line straight up and down, but even then, you'll hang up once in a while. Here's how to improve your chances of freeing a lure if you do get snagged. Use a longer rod so you can reach out farther to change your angle of pull, making it possible to dislodge the hook without repositioning the boat. Some anglers use specially designed spinning rods up to 8 feet long or they rig a fly rod with a spinning reel.

SLIP IN ON WALLEYES

The sound of an outboard, the whir of an electric trolling motor, or the clunk of an anchor can spook walleyes off a shallow reef. To approach such a spot silently, anchor at least 50 feet upwind, and pay out rope until you're within casting range. If you need to check the reef with your depth finder, let your boat blow right over the spot, take your readings, and then move slightly upwind by taking in anchor rope.

SPRINGTIME WALLEYE MAGNET

Walleye fishermen know that the fish feed in the shallows in spring because the water there is warmer than in the main body of the lake. The difference may be only a degree or two, but it's enough to attract baitfish, and the walleyes soon follow.

But some areas along shore are warmer than others, so they draw more walleyes. Water in a sheltered bay, for instance, warms faster than water along a straight shoreline because the wind can't mix it with deeper, cooler water.

Bays are obvious spots to check, but here's another type of spot that's not so obvious:

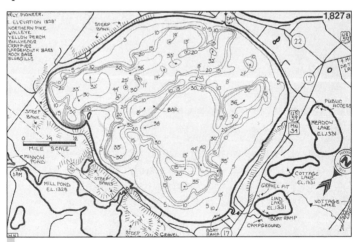

INDENTATIONS in the breakline function much like bays, but are not obvious from looking at the shoreline. Sunlight heats the surface layer of the lake, and if the wind pushes the warm water toward shore, it will collect in the depression. An indentation on the downwind side of the lake may have water 10 degrees warmer than nearby shallows.

SLOW DOWN SLIP-BOBBERS

Slip-bobbers are tough to beat when fishing live bait for walleyes. A breeze can make the rig even more effective by slowly moving the bobber and bait through water that might hold fish. Yet a strong wind will move the bobber and bait too fast to interest any but the most active fish. Here are some ways to slow down the drift and catch walleyes that aren't willing to chase a fast-moving bait:

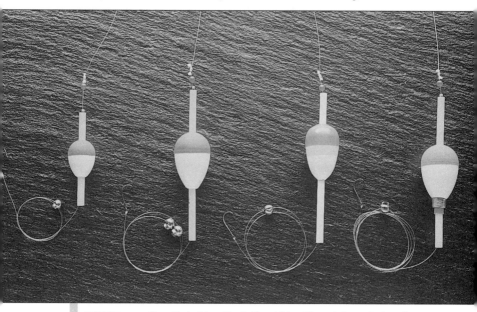

SELECT a smaller slip bobber (far left), which will catch less wind and move the bait more slowly than a large float. USE enough weight on your line (middle left) that the bobber barely floats; this way it is little affected by wind. CHOOSE a wooden float (middle right); it's denser than foam so it rides lower, drifts slower and casts better. USE a bobber weighted with a lead sleeve (far right). It will ride low and drift slowly, and the extra weight will increase casting distance.

THERE'S MORE THAN ONE WAY TO HOOK A LEECH

Most fishermen hook their leeches in or around the sucker, the large disc on the wide end (tail). This method of hooking works well for most types of fishing, but there are times when other ways are more effective.

Here are the best ways to hook leeches for various fishing situations:

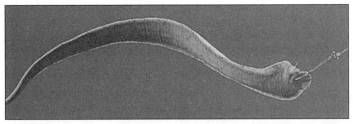

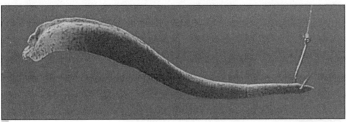

THROUGH THE SUCKER (top). Hooking in or near the sucker is recommended for most casting and trolling. Because you pull the leech backwards, it always tries to swim away.

THROUGH THE NECK (middle). This method is best when nipping panfish are a problem. The flesh in the neck region is very tough, making it harder for them to steal your bait.

THROUGH THE MIDDLE (bottom). This method is ideal for bobber fishing. The leech is balanced on the hook, so it undulates more than it would if hooked in the end.

CURE FOR BALLED-UP LEECHES

When the water is cold (below 50°F), leeches tend to ball up on the hook (inset). Even in warm water, a leech occasionally decides to roll itself up tight. Regardless of what you do, you can't get them to unwind and swim. The problem occurs most often when the leech is hooked through the neck, though some leeches ball up no matter where you hook them. Unfortunately, a balled-up leech is worthless for walleyes.

Prevent the problem by sliding a short piece of surgical tubing over the collar of the jig. Hook the leech far enough ahead of the sucker so the sucker can attach to the tubing. A leech with its sucker attached to something is not as likely to ball up.

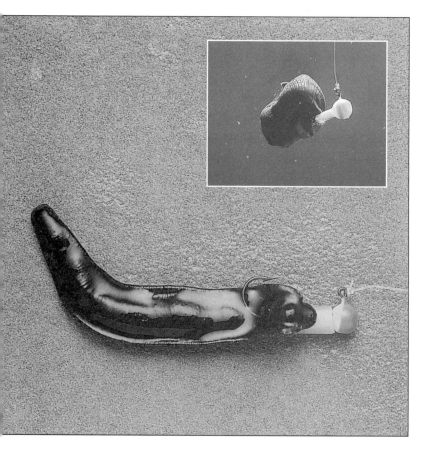

FREE-STANDING STINGER

Walleyes often nip at a jig and minnow without getting hooked. Many anglers tie a small treble to the bend of the jig hook and imbed this "stinger" in the minnow's tail. But even light mono between the jig and treble inhibits the action of the bait. And the line often wraps around the minnow, cinching it into a half-circle and ruining its action. Here's a better way.

Tie a size 14 or 16 treble hook to the bend of the jig hook with a short length of stiff line, such as Mason hard mono, 15-pound test or heavier. The stiff line holds the treble straight out behind the jig, so you don't need to hook it in the minnow. The bait moves freely, as if the stinger weren't there at all. Yet when a fish nips the tail, it gets hooked.

CUT THROUGH STRINGY WEEDS

Walleyes are sometimes found in stringy weeds, such as coontail. The weeds catch on your line, slide down and foul your lure. Sometimes you can shake them off during the retrieve, but more often you have to reel in the lure and remove the weeds by hand. Here's an easier way.

Add a short leader of thin multistrand wire, such as 12-pound-test Sevenstrand, between your line and lure. When you feel resistance from a weed, jerk the rod. The thin wire will cut through the stem, and the weed will fall off the line. The wire leader also ensures that sharp-toothed fish such as northern pike won't bite off your lure.

DURABLE NATURAL JIG DRESSING

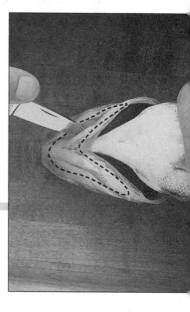

If you run out of bait and walleyes refuse artificials, try tipping a jig with throat tissue cut from a walleye you've already caught. The thin flesh wiggles enticingly on the hook, emits natural scent and is remarkably durable.

When you clean a batch of walleyes, cut out these throat pieces and freeze them for later use. Here's how:

CUT out the throat tissue by slicing along the dotted lines as shown. Then cut the tissue loose at the point of the chin. Drive the jig hook through the front of the piece of throat tissue. The meat there is thicker and tough, so the hook won't tear out.

EARLY-BIRD WALLEYES

Walleyes in heavily used lakes often feed earlier in the day than those in less popular lakes. Speedboaters, jet-skiers, water-skiers and other commotion drive them into deep water or heavy cover. Often, the traffic stays heavy until dark, and walleyes don't feed much before the lake settles down.

To catch these early feeders, start fishing at the crack of dawn. The bite may end by breakfast time.

CLEAN JIG EYES

Most jigs you buy are painted by dipping the entire head. Usually the attachment eye is clogged with paint, so you have to poke a hole to attach your line. But if you use another hook to open the eye, as many anglers do, some paint will remain on the eye. When you tie on your jig, the knot won't snug up properly, and the rough edge can fray your line. To avoid these problems, clean out the eye like this:

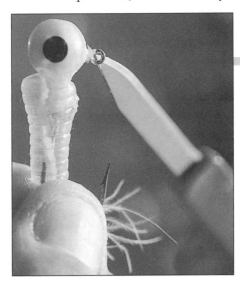

PUSH the point of a knife blade into the eye and give it a half twist. Usually, all of the paint will chip away from the eye. If not, scrape away any that is left to make a smooth surface for your knot.

CHART DEPTH WHILE ICE FISHING

Often walleyes will school on a small point or in a tiny indentation along the breakline. It takes a lot of depth readings to find these spots, and even then, you may not get a clear picture of the bottom unless you keep track of the depth at each location.

After you sound through the ice or through an ice hole, use the handle of your ice scoop to scratch the depth in the ice or snow. You can even stomp contour lines in the snow, joining holes of equal depths.

Once you have marked the depths and contours, you will have a much better understanding of the structure and where fish might be.

IMPROVED WILLOW RIG

Veteran walleye and sauger anglers often use a willow twig to detect subtle bites while ice fishing. They anchor a 2- to 3-foot twig in the slush removed from the hole, then center the tip over the hole, about a foot above the water. Then they make a loop in the line and hang it over the tip of the twig. A light bite pulls the willow down slightly; a hard bite bends the willow far enough down so the loop slips off.

Normally, line is spread on the ice so the fish can run with no resistance.

But the loop often catches on the end of the willow, and the loose line sometimes catches on ice chips. The fish feel the resistance and drop the bait. Here's how to overcome these problems:

THREAD a light float on the line and drape the float over the tip of the twig. The minnow will not be strong enough to dislodge the float, but a firm strike will pull it free. Set a small spool of mono in a shallow circular depression you've formed in the snow or chopped in the ice. As a fish takes line, the spool will spin in the cavity until you grab the line and set the hook.

DON'T DRILL AT DUSK

Many ice fishermen make the mistake of showing up at dusk, just when the walleyes are moving in to feed. When they drill their holes, they spook the fish. You can avoid the problem by drilling your holes an hour earlier.

Northern Pike & Muskie Tips

ADD FLASH TO MUSKIE LURES

Muskies are notorious for following lures to the boat and turning away at the last minute without striking. If you are getting follows but no strikes, try dressing up the lure with a small spinner. The added flash and vibration is often all it takes to trigger a strike. Here's how to add spinners to three different kinds of lures:

JERKBAITS with metal tail blades, such as Suicks, can be modified by drilling a small hole at the center of the rear edge of the tail blade. Add a split ring, a snap-swivel and a size 0, 1 or 2 spinner. The greater drag of sizes larger than this inhibits the lure's action. The snap allows you to easily remove or change the spinner blade.

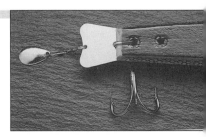

GLIDEBAITS and other jerkbaits without metal tail blades, such as Reef Hawgs and Eddie Baits, can also be fitted with a spinner blade. Remove the rear treble hook. Then replace it with a split ring, a snap-swivel and a size 0, 1 or 2 spinner blade.

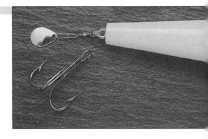

CREATURES, such as big soft-plastic water-dog imitations, can be modified by threading a long needle with 10-pound mono (top) into the "chest" of the creature and out the tail. If you can't find a needle long enough to do the job, use a piece of stiff piano wire with a loop in one end. PULL the needle and line out the tip of the tail (upper middle). TIE line to a snap-swivel and number 1, 2 or 3 spinner (lower middle). PULL the swivel snug to the end of the tail (bottom). Insert a large jig with a stout hook into the head of the lure; tie off the line on the bend of the hook.

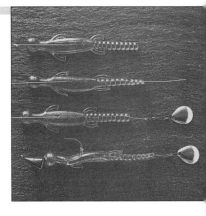

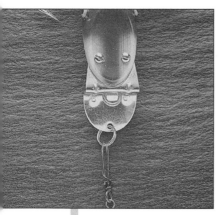

WEED-RESISTANT PIKE PLUGS

Pike are suckers for big, metal-lipped plugs such as Pikie Minnows, but when the fish are lurking in shallow weeds, these plugs are impossible to use. They run too deep, and the lip collects weeds.

Here's a way to modify these plugs so they run shallower and don't pick up as many weeds:

DRILL a hole near the end of the lip and insert a split ring; attach your leader. The plug will run just under the surface. And weeds will slip down the line and pass under the plug, rather than hang up on the lip.

MUSKIES AFTER DARK

Boat traffic and fishing pressure can force muskies to feed at night. Successful fishermen change their habits, too. Fish the same areas you would during the day, and try shallower areas as well. Use bucktails or jointed plugs, working them with a steady retrieve so the fish can easily home in on them.

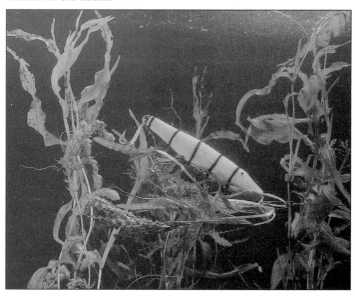

GO DEEP FOR BIG SUMMERTIME PIKE

Fishermen catch plenty of good-sized pike in shallow weedy bays in spring, but when the water warms up, they get nothing but "hammer handles" in these areas. The lack of big pike in summer had led to the mistaken belief that big pike lose their teeth or have sore mouths in summer and don't feed. But in reality, they're feeding more than ever.

The main reason for the scarcity of big pike in summer is that anglers aren't fishing deep enough. As pike get larger, they prefer cooler water. In some cases, they'll stay in shallow water and congregate around spring holes, artesian wells, the mouths of trout streams, or other specific point sources of cold water. But if there are no point sources, pike have no choice but to go deep.

If there is adequate oxygen in the lake depths, they'll go as deep as 50 feet and occasionally down to 100. Lake trout anglers sometimes catch big pike. At these depths, they're generally feeding on good-sized baitfish, such as ciscoes and whitefish, and you'll have to use similar-sized baits to catch them.

IMPROVE GLIDEBAIT ACTION

A wire leader deadens the action of a glidebait, such as an Eddie Bait or Reef Hawg. But you can increase the glide and the side-to-side motion by inserting a split ring between the leader and the bait. The ring allows freer play between the steel leader loop and the eye of the plug.

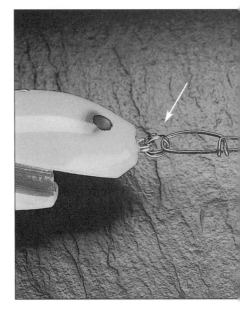

If you're using heavy line and are concerned about the strength of the connection, solder the ring, making sure to file all rough edges that would inhibit movement of the lure. Or you can fit a small split ring inside a larger one.

WEIGHT BUCKTAILS QUICKLY

Fishermen often weight bucktails to make them run deeper or to cast farther into a stiff wind. But sinkers added to the line makes casting awkward; the sinker and lure twirl like a bolo. You can eliminate tangles by adding weight directly to the lure. Here's how:

ATTACH a Snap-Lac bell sinker of the appropriate weight to the split ring or wire loop that holds the treble hook. These sinkers make changing or removing weight easy.

PROTECT HANDS FROM SHARP TEETH

The needle-sharp teeth of pike and muskies, and the large hooks you use to catch these fish, are a constant danger and can inflict serious wounds in an instant. Protect your hands with heavy buck-skin gloves while landing and unhooking these fish. The hooks aren't likely to penetrate the thick leather.

SPLIT RINGS IMPROVE HOOKING

Muskies and big pike often manage to throw the hook by twisting and thrashing against the weight of a plug. Improve your chances of landing the fish by inserting split rings between the lure and trebles. The rings allow the hooks freer play so big fish can't twist free or bend hooks as easily. Here's how to add them:

CUT off the old treble hooks or remove them by opening the eye of the hook hanger.

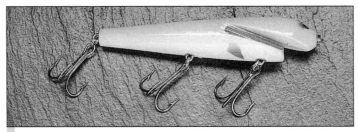

ADD split rings or double split rings (p. 120) and new trebles; close the eye of the hook hanger.

BUCKTAILS WITH SPICE

More muskies are caught on bucktails than on any other lure. But here's a way to make bucktails work even better:

ADD a split ring and snap to the wire loop holding the rear treble. Clip a 2-inch white split-tail pork rind onto the snap. If necessary, trim the rind at the leading end and punch a new hole. The rind should stick only 1/2 inch beyond the bucktail. If you attach the rind directly to the treble and it trails back too far, muskies may strike short.

A STINGER FOR PIKE PLUGS

When a big pike or muskie grabs a large wooden plug, it's difficult to get a good hook set because their teeth penetrate the wood, preventing you from moving the plug enough to sink the hooks. Here's a way to rig a large plug that will improve your chances of hooking pike and muskies:

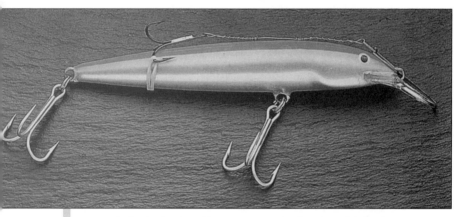

RIG a 4-inch wire leader with a snap at one end and a treble hook at the other. Clip the snap to the eye at the nose of the lure. Lay the treble along the plug's back and secure the hook with a rubber band. The treble should be big enough to hold a large fish, but not heavy enough to throw the plug out of balance.

MORE HOOKUPS ON JERKBAITS

Jerkbaits account for plenty of good-sized pike and muskies, especially in fall. But many fishermen work jerkbaits too erratically. They sweep the rod 3 to 4 feet at a time, causing the lure to dodge rapidly from side to side. As a result, fish often miss the lure. Here's a better way.

Work the lure with smooth, slow and regular 2-foot sweeps of the rod tip. The lure will still have enough swimming action to attract pike and muskies, but they'll have an easier time catching it, and you'll get more hookups.

CONTINUOUS FIGURE EIGHT

This unique two-person procedure has produced dozens of 30-pound-plus fish for northern Wisconsin muskie experts. It would work for muskies anywhere.

While one person casts, another figure-eights alongside the boat. When the first person completes his retrieve, he starts figure-eighting, and the other person makes a cast. This way, someone is figure-eighting at all times.

The continuous motion evidently arouses the curiosity of big muskies. Even fish that haven't been seen following the lure being retrieved will suddenly appear and strike the figure-eighted lure.

FINER POINTS OF FIGURE-EIGHTING

Muskies are notorious for following a lure to the boat. Good muskie anglers know how to figure-eight a lure to get the fish to strike. But the technique involves more than just sweeping the rod back and forth through the water. Done poorly, figure-eights result in little more than good arm exercise. Done right, they can more than double your muskie catch. Here are some tricks the experts recommend:

- Use a heavy-duty baitcasting reel with the drag set tight. When a muskie follows your lure to the boat, thumb the spool and push in the free-spool button. Then, should a big fish strike next to the boat, you can set the hook and give line when the fish runs.

- When you see a muskie behind your lure, it's important to read its mood to determine how to proceed. If the fish is "hot," you stand a good chance of enticing it to strike. But if it's only mildly interested, you may be better off leaving it alone.

- Watch the fish's head; if it stays within a few inches of the lure and the mouth is opening and closing, the fish is hot. Begin tracing a big figure eight with the rod tip. The lure should be about 2 feet underwater. If the fish continues to follow but doesn't strike, bring the lure back over its snout. This maneuver often triggers a strike.

• If you see a fish following a few feet behind the lure and swimming lazily, chances are it's not ready to strike. You may want to try one or two figure eights, but if the fish doesn't respond, don't continue. You may end up spooking the fish. Instead, note the precise location. Then come back and try again later. By that time, the fish may be in a more aggressive mood.

• To make a muskie take the lure, do everything you can to keep it away. Many fishermen make the mistake of slowing the lure when they see a fish following, but this is a sure way to make the fish lose interest. Slow down only when the fish quits following, then speed up again. Sometimes the change in speeds will bring the fish back.

• If a muskie follows a surface lure to the boat, don't figure-eight the lure on top. It's nearly always a waste of time. Even if you're using a surface crawler with no underwater action at all, plunge the rod tip into the water and figure-eight the lure a couple feet beneath the surface.

BETTER HOOK SETS WITH BIG BAITS

Anglers sometimes use suckers more than a foot long to catch trophy pike and muskies. These baitfish are usually hooked through the nose, but the thick snout of a really large sucker fills up the hook gap and makes a good hook set difficult. On page 73 are two ways to rig these big baitfish so the hook point remains exposed and the bait stays alive. With either of these methods, you'll have to pause long enough for the fish to swallow the bait before attempting to set the hook.

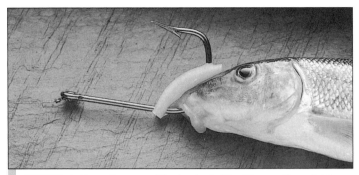

METHOD 1: Open the gap of the hook slightly; this way the point is more likely to hook a fish and less likely to get buried in the bait. Thread on a "keeper" made of a strip of surgical tubing or a heavy rubber band to keep the sucker from sliding up and down the hook shank. Hook the sucker upward through the snout only, not both lips, to keep more of the hook point exposed. Finally, slide the other end of the rubber keeper onto the hook.

METHOD 2: Thread a large needle with a foot of heavy braided Dacron fishing line. (1) Push the needle through the eye sockets of the sucker. Draw the line through the head of the bait, and (2) tie the ends together to form a loose loop. Trim the ends. (3) Insert a large hook in the loop and twist it several times so the line tightens across the head of the bait. (4) Slip the hook under the taut line and adjust it so the point rides up.

SPOKES FOR SPINNERS

A lot of muskie and pike fishermen make their own spinnerbaits and in-line spinners. Most of the components are readily available from specialty fishing tackle stores and mail-order firms. But you may have trouble finding the stiff, heavy stainless steel wire (at least .060 inch) you need to make really large spinners and spinnerbaits. If the wire is too light, fish will bend it and the spinners won't spin properly. A ready source of heavy wire: bicycle wheel spokes. The rustproof spokes are available in any bicycle shop.

KEEPING THE KINKS OUT

Many anglers use twisted multistrand steel leaders to keep pike and muskies from biting through the line. But these leaders easily get kinks that are impossible to remove. Then, as you work a lure, the leader flexes at the kink, eventually weakening and perhaps breaking as you play a fish. Get around the problem this way. Buy single-strand leaders or make them yourself from stainless steel wire. It kinks less than twisted wire, and kinks that do form are easier to remove. As a result, a leader that is no heavier remains stronger.

JERKING LIVE BAIT FOR PIKE

This unusual but effective method for big pike and muskies combines the action of a jerkbait with the appeal of live bait.

Hook a 6- to 10-inch sucker minnow upward through only the snout with a 2/0 to 5/0 short-shanked bait hook attached to a foot-long wire leader. Cast the minnow with a heavy baitcasting or spinning outfit.

Retrieve the sucker with 2-foot jerks, occasionally pausing to let the bait glide and roll. When you see or feel a strike, wait until you think the fish has swallowed the bait before setting the hook.

Where it is legal, you can rig a small treble hook as a stinger, joining it to the eye of the other hook with a 6-inch section of wire. Hook one prong of the treble in the tail. With this rig, set the hook immediately.

When it is necessary to sink the bait several feet, pinch a large split-shot to the wire leader, several inches above the nose of the sucker.

PREVENT BAIT TANGLES

Monofilament line absorbs water and sinks, sometimes causing problems for bobber fishermen. When you fish a big minnow below a bobber, the bait may swim near the surface, crossing the submerged line between the rod tip and bobber and causing a tangled mess. Even if the sucker doesn't cause a tangle, the sag in the line may prevent a good hook set. You can solve the problem by applying candle wax or fly floatant to the line. The mono will float and stay out of the way of the swimming baitfish.

Trout & Salmon Tips

WORMIN' FOR SALMON

During their life at sea, chinooks, cohos and other Pacific salmon eat small eels of various kinds. Once the salmon enter rivers to spawn, they no longer feed, but they still strike lures resembling eels. As a result, they can be caught on the curly-tailed worms normally used for bass.

Hook a 3- to 5-inch worm on a stout-hooked jig heavy enough to run just off the bottom. Bright or fluorescent colors are usually best, but black and purple work well on bright days.

Anchor your boat above a holding area, then angle your cast down and across the river. Let the current swing the worm in front of the salmon. Or troll the worm through deep water on bends or by creek mouths. Salmon usually hit these lures hard; set the hook as soon as you feel the strike.

PEANUTS GIVE BAIT A LIFT

Lake trout will take dead smelt or ciscoes lying on the bottom, but these baits are more effective when floated up a foot or two. Because lakers are usually found in very deep water, using a slip bobber to suspend the bait is not practical.

Here's a way to float dead bait just off the bottom, where it's visible and appears to be barely alive. It works not only for lakers, but also for big pike.

STUFF a (1) Styrofoam packing peanut inside the mouth of the bait and (2) run the hook through both lips to keep the mouth shut. If more flotation is needed to make the bait float, (3) cut a small slit in the belly and stuff another peanut or two into the abdomen. If the bait is small, use pieces of a peanut. (4) Slip a rubber band over the fish or tie mono around the bait to keep the peanut in the body. Fish the bait 2 feet behind a ¹/₂- to 1-ounce sinker.

EASY-TO-SEE STRIKE INDICATORS

Even fluorescent strike indicators can be tough to see in cloudy or hazy weather when you're squinting into the brightest part of the sky. Here's a solution:

COLOR one end of a strike indicator with a black waterproof marker to provide a dark silhouette. Now, in any light, at least half of the indicator will be visible.

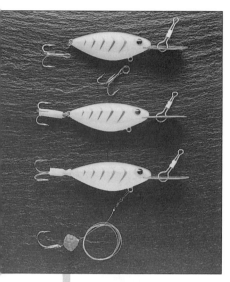

DOUBLE-DUTY STEELHEAD PLUG

West Coast steelheaders often use a crankbait, such as a magnum Hot 'N Tot, to carry bait to the bottom of a steelhead run and also to act as an attractor. Normally, the hooks are removed so they don't foul the trailing bait rig. But then you miss the occasional steelhead that strikes the plug.

Here's a way of rigging the crankbait so you can catch fish on the plug as well as the bait:

REMOVE the front treble and split ring (top); then remove the rear treble, leaving the split ring on the plug. SLIDE a short piece of surgical tubing (middle) over the rear hook shank and then reattach the hook. SLIDE the tubing forward (bottom) so it covers the rear eye, split ring and hook eye, and fasten the desired bait rig to the front eye. The tubing will cause the treble hook to stick straight off the rear of the plug so it won't foul the trailing bait rig.

KEEP REELS DRY WHEN WADING

Wading anglers who fish with a fly rod or long spinning rod are familiar with the problem: to unwrap line from the rod tip or restring the tip section of the rod, you must dunk the reel in the water to reach the last few guides. But then sand gets in your reel. Immersion also causes the drags of some reels to slip.

You can avoid these problems by pulling the rod apart at the ferrule. Now you can untangle the line from the end of the rod or string up the tip section without putting the reel in the water.

BETTER FLY FLOATANT

Silicon gel fly pastes are handy but are difficult to apply to flies evenly and thoroughly. If you don't apply enough, the fly won't float long. If you dab on too much, the hackles, wings and tail mat down. What you need is a dressing that cleans and treats every part of the fly, evaporates quickly, and floats a fly a long time. Here's how to make a dressing that does just that:

MIX one part silicon gel fly floatant with three parts lighter fluid. Store the mixture in a small jar or squeeze bottle, after first adding a little to the bottle to make sure the plastic doesn't dissolve. Squeeze a drop or two directly onto the fly or apply it with your fingers or a toothpick. The lighter fluid will evaporate in seconds, leaving a thin coat of the gel on the hackles and body of the fly.

ICE JIGS SCORE IN STREAMS

If you're fishing worms for stream trout, you'll generally need a bit of weight to aid casting and get the worm down to the fish. Pinching a split-shot or two several inches above the bait does the trick, but the shot and hook will revolve around one another on the cast, making accurate placement diffi-cult. Here's a way to make your bait easier to cast and also more appealing to the fish:

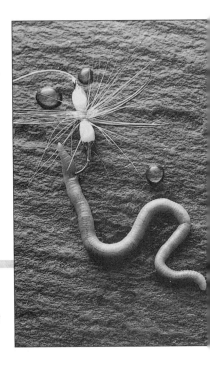

HOOK the worm on a gold, silver or fluo-rescent panfish ice fly. For best casting, use 2- or 4-pound mono on an ultralight spinning rig. The ice fly and worm will cast as a unit, improving your accuracy.

SKI WAX TAMES DUBBING

Spinning short animal hair onto a thread, a process called "dubbing," is the first step in forming the bodies of many dry flies, wet flies and nymphs. However, the process can be tricky and messy, especially for a beginning fly tier, because short hair doesn't adhere very well to the thread. Instead, it sticks to the tier's fingers or falls into his lap.

Here's a way to make the hair stick so it's easier to spin onto the thread:

APPLY a light coating of soft (warm-weather) cross-country ski wax to several inches of thread (left). DAB on the hair (right). Pinch the thread below the hair; roll the thread between your thumb and forefinger to form yarn.

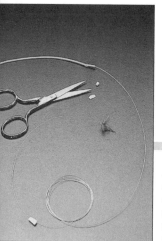

WATCHING HARD-TO-SEE FLIES

It's important to watch the drift of a dry fly so you can detect strikes and set the hook. But there are times glare or darkness makes it hard to see dry flies, especially those that imitate small naturals, such as midges. The next time poor lighting makes dry-fly fishing difficult, try this trick:

WRAP half of an adhesive foam strike indicator (the kind used by nymph fishermen) around the tippet, about 10 inches above the fly. Trim it to the size of a BB so it doesn't hinder casting or spook fish. This small piece of white foam will be much easier to follow in poor light than a tiny, dark fly. When a fish takes the fly, the foam disappears.

A SHOULDER TO LEAN ON

Slippery rocks and swift water can make wading treacherous. If you're fishing a stream with a friend, wade across fast riffles or runs while gripping each other's vest or jacket. Your footing and balance will be much surer than if you had tried to wade alone.

STOPPING A STRONG RUN

When hooked, a big salmon or steelhead makes a swift, powerful run, sometimes stripping off a hundred yards of line or more. If you're fishing in a boat, you may have no choice but to turn around and chase the fish. When wading in a stream, you may have to follow the fish downstream. If you can't, it will break off in seconds. Here's a trick that will stop a streaking fish nine times out of ten.

Give the fish complete slack. They run because they feel resistance; when there is no resistance, they usually stop. In a stream, they often swim back upriver. Once you gain back some line, you can put the pressure on again.

FIND TROUT LIES QUICKLY

Fly fishermen can improve their success by learning where
the trout are before they start fishing. Catch a few terrestrial
insects, such as grasshoppers, crickets or beetles. Toss them
into the stream and watch them carefully. When a trout grabs
one, note the location so you'll know where to cast your fly.

DACRON BACKING SAVES FLY REELS

Steelheaders often drift flies or bait along the bottom in
swift current using a long fly rod rigged with monofilament. The line is stripped off by hand rather than cast off
the reel. Many anglers prefer a fly reel to a spinning reel,
because the loose loops that form when lobbing and drifting a bait are less likely to tangle on its smaller handle and
more compact form. But don't fill a fly reel only with
monofilament. Mono stretches under the tension of loading the line or reeling in a fish. Then it constricts on the
spool, exerting force not only against the arbor but the
sides of the spool as well. This sideways force may cause
the spool to spread and bind against the frame.

To avoid ruining your fly reel, fill it to within 1/2 inch of the
pillars with braided Dacron line, which stretches very little.
Top off the spool with about 100 yards of 8- to 12-pound
mono, joining the mono to the Dacron as shown below:

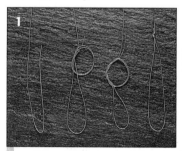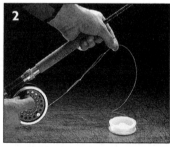

*1. TIE a double surgeon's loop in the end of each line by (left to right)
doubling over the line, tying an overhand knot with the loop, and pushing the loop through the knot a second time. Pull tight and clip the end.*

*2. INTERLOCK the two loops by threading the mono loop through the
Dacron loop and then passing the mono spool through the mono loop.
Pull the loops tight. Then fill your reel with mono to within 1/8 inch of
the pillars.*

PRETIED TIPPETS SAVE TIME

Some predictable mayfly hatches occur late in the evening. The hatch – and the fishing – can turn on suddenly and proceed at a furious pace. When it's dark and the fish are feeding aggressively, it's easy to break off a fly on a fish or snag it in the brush. Because these hatches may peak and end within minutes, the time-consuming task of trying to tie on a small fly in the dark is especially frustrating. And even a small flashlight can ruin what night vision you do have.

Here's how a little preparation at home can save time and prevent frustration once you're on the stream:

ATTACH 2-foot tippets to several flies of the pattern you think you'll need. Tie a double surgeon's loop in the other end of each tippet. Coil the tippets and tuck them in your hat band, sandwich them in a Velcro fastener on your vest, or hook the flies in a fleece patch and let the tippets dangle. Tie a double surgeon's loop in the end of your leader, and loop on one of the pretied tippets and flies. This way, if you break off a fly, you can simply replace the tippet. Changing tippets is much faster and easier than tying on small flies – especially if it's dark and you're surrounded by hungry trout.

"UNMATCH" THE HATCH TO TAKE TROUT

Sometimes, even dedicated match-the-hatch fly fishermen have to admit defeat. If trout refuse a fly intended to match the insects on the water, here's a trick that may provoke a strike.

Instead of dead-drifting a dry fly, give it a twitch or two, or let the line belly out so the fly skates across the surface. Another option: try a fly that differs from the naturals in size, shape and color.

Trout will closely inspect and often reject a fly that is almost, but not quite, identical to the insect that is hatching. But they will hit something that is completely different.

ADD YARN TO AN EGG LOOP

Fresh spawn with a bit of bright yarn is a top steelhead and salmon bait. Most anglers snell the eggs and yarn on the hook. But a snell (opposite page) may pinch off the eggs. An egg loop won't pinch off spawn, but it doesn't draw tight enough to hold the yarn. Here's how you can add yarn to an egg loop:

Tie an egg loop by threading the end of a 24- inch piece of mono through a hook with an upturned eye. Wrap the long end around the shank and tag end six to eight times. Make a loop, then push the long end back through the eye. Hold the wrapped portion while making six or eight more wraps over the tag end and the other line. Insert a small bunch of yarn in the rear loop, and then pull on the long end of the line to tighten the knot and secure the yarn. Trim the tag end of the line. Grasp the yarn in a single bunch and clip it with a scissors to form an egglike ball. Cut a marble-sized ball of spawn from a skein of fresh salmon eggs, leaving as much of the membrane as possible to hold the eggs together. Open the front loop of the knot, slip the eggs inside, and pull the loop tight, securing the eggs to the hook. The knot won't pinch off the eggs, yet the rear loop will hold the yarn firmly in place.

"POPPING" A LURE CAN BRING A STRIKE

A sudden change in the action, speed and direction of a trolled lure can cause a salmon or trout to strike, but when fishing with downriggers, it's tough to vary the action of the lures. If you have no luck trolling through a school of fish that shows on your graph, try this: Jerk on the rod to pop the lure from the downrigger release. Then do nothing. Let the lure rise and trail near the surface for a moment. The sudden change in the action often draws a strike. After popping the release, you must raise the ball to re-rig, so it's a technique to use mainly when you will be lifting the ball to change or inspect the lures.

OFFBEAT COLORS FOR STEELHEAD

When drift-fishing for steelhead or salmon, many fishermen use bright or fluorescent yarn. Fish probably mistake these flies for spawn. But don't limit yourself to old standards, such as orange, pink and chartreuse. Here are some other colors and color combinations that often work when the usual colors don't.

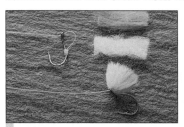 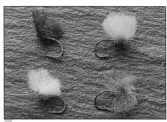

INSERT two pieces of contrasting yarn (top) into the loop of a snelled egg hook. PULL the line to cinch up the yarn (bottom), then trim so the yarn is 1/4 to 3/4 inch long. The two-toned pattern may catch fish when neither color alone draws a strike.

MAKE a fly from black, tan or brown yarn. These flies don't resemble spawn at all, but rather natural foods, such as stonefly and mayfly nymphs. Also effective at times is blue yarn, though it resembles nothing steelhead or salmon would normally eat.

NO-CLING GUIDES FOR DRIFT FISHING

When you drift yarn or spawn for steelhead or salmon, it pays to use as long a rod as possible. A long rod holds the line off the water better than a short one, making it easier to control line during the drift. But if you use a fly rod and mono, as many anglers do, the snake guides let the line slap against the rod shaft. In rainy weather, the mono clings to the wet rod, cutting the cast short. You can avoid the problem by modifying your existing fly rod or building a new one especially for drift-fishing. Here's how:

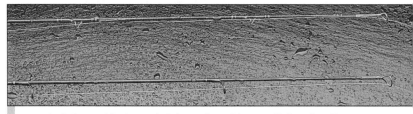

USE single-foot guides instead of the snake guides usually found on fly rods. The single-foots do a better job of holding the wet line away from the rod shaft. The result: your line zips through the guides with less drag.

GET A GRIP ON SALMON

Anglers wade-fishing streams for Atlantic or chinook salmon often have to fight through brush and hike over rough terrain to reach their fishing spots. A large landing net catches in brush and is a pain to carry.

Some fishermen choose to leave the nets at home and "tail" their salmon by leading the fish close, grabbing the base of its tail and quickly lifting. Atlantics and chinooks have stiff outer rays in the tail that keep it from folding and slipping through your fingers. Tailing is often used for fish up to about 20 pounds, though the size you can handle will depend on practice and the strength of your grip.

To get the surest grip on your prize before you lift, try this trick:

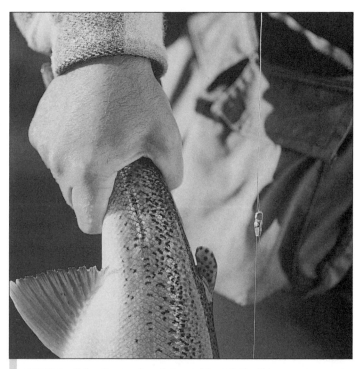

GRASP the fish with your thumb toward the tail. You'll have a strong grip and your arm will be in a good position to lift. If you grab the fish with your thumb toward the fish's head, you will be forced to lift in an awkward, backhanded manner. Your grip won't be as strong and the tail is more likely to slip out of your hand.

"CHEATER" INCREASES ODDS

When using downriggers, more lures mean more fish. But that requires extra rods. Here's a way to fish two lures on a rod, each at a different depth, by using a "cheater":

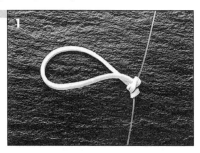

1. LOOP a rubber band to your line after letting it out, attaching it to a release and lowering the cannonball down about 10 feet. To prevent the rubber band from slipping, wrap it around the line twice, pushing one loop through the other, and cinch it tight.

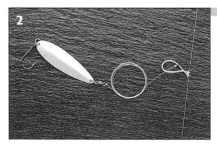

2. RIG a cheater by running one end of an 8-foot mono leader with a second lure through the rubber band; clip the leader snap to your line. The rubber band keeps the leader from sliding up and down.

3. LOWER the downrigger ball to the desired depth. When a fish strikes, the rubber band breaks. The cheater snap slides down the main line, pops the release, and continues sliding until it jams against the lower lure. Now you have a direct pull on the fish.

STACK THE RIGHT SPOONS

Stacking spoons on downriggers (attaching two or three spoons on the same downrigger cable) is one of the best ways to improve your odds of catching salmon. But anglers who stack spoons of different weights risk tangling their lines unless they know how to arrange their spoons properly.

If you want to stack heavy trolling spoons along with light spoons, always run the heaviest spoons closest to the bottom. If you stack heavy spoons above the light ones, the heavy spoons will sink faster when you make a turn or slow down, fouling the lines that go to the light spoons.

AN ANT FOR ALL SEASONS

If rising trout won't take an exact imitation of the insects that are emerging, try this trick.

Tie on a black ant pattern that is smaller than the insects the trout are eating. Cast upstream and fish the ant on a dead drift. Trout that reject exact imitations will often take small ant patterns, even during winter and early spring, when no real ants can be found. In fact, the trick of using a fly that's smaller than the natural works with other patterns, too.

When matching a hatch with a dry fly, it's usually better to use a size smaller than you think you should. Why? First, we overestimate the size of insects in the air. Second, the hackle of a dry fly makes it look larger than a natural with the same length body and wing.

FOLLOW SHIFTING PLUMES

Big-lake salmon and trout anglers know that the fish are strongly attracted to plumes of water flowing into the lake from rivers and even very small creeks. These plumes carry the scent of the streams where the fish hatched or were stocked. The river water also creates a mixing zone in the lake where the water temperature is often ideal.

But many fishermen do not realize that winds can shift the plumes around. One day the plume is blown north, the next day south. The fish follow the plumes as the wind moves them about. So if you fish the same area day after day, you may be on fish one day and nowhere near them the next.

You can locate these shifting plumes by looking for the change in color between lake and river water. But sometimes, the change is hard to see. If the river is large, you may be able to find the plume with the help of a surface-temperature gauge. A small creek, however, has too little flow to have much effect on the lake temperature. In that case, try to anticipate where wind will blow the creek water. Be sure to fish the windy side of downwind points and piers, where the water is most likely to collect.

SNAGPROOF SALMON FLIES

Standard salmon streamers and wet flies are tied to ride with the wing up and the hook point down. But a fly tied this way hangs up easily and is likely to snag a salmon if the leader drifts over the fish's back during the retrieve.

 Fighting foul-hooked salmon takes time better spent fishing, and if you break off, you lose leaders and flies. Even if you don't foul-hook the fish, it may feel the hook across its back and dart away. Here's a trick some fly fishermen have borrowed from saltwater anglers to avoid snagging bottom or the fish:

TIE your favorite streamer patterns upside down, like bonefish flies. The hook rides point up and is protected by the wing

CHEAP NO-SLIP SOLES

The algae-covered boulders in some trout streams are as slick as grease. With ordinary rubber-soled boots you can fall flat on your face. Many anglers buy expensive boots or waders with felt soles to get traction on slippery rocks, but here's a cheap way to improve your footing with waders you already own:

*1. GRIND the lugs off the soles of your boots with a coarse-grained belt or disk sander to provide a roughed-up but flat surface for gluing.
2. TRACE the outline of the boots onto a scrap of indoor-outdoor carpet. Scrape any foam backing off the carpet soles with a wire brush.
3. COAT the sole and carpet with a strong adhesive. Follow the directions that come with the glue. Tape on the soles until the adhesive sets.*

INTERCHANGEABLE SINKING TIPS

Many fly fishermen use sink-tip lines to get streamers or nymphs down to trout feeding near the bottom in a fast run. The sink rate and length of the sinking portion varies from line to line. The best combination for one situation won't necessarily be the best choice in another. You could solve the problem by carrying several different sink-tip lines. But here's a cheaper and more convenient way:

1. CUT lead-core line in several lengths from 18 inches to 6 feet long. Form small loops on the end of each piece, just as you would on the end of a fly line.

2. LOOP a section of lead core between your fly line and a 3-foot mono leader. Use a short piece to sink a fly in shallow water, a longer one in deeper water.

Panfish Tips

FINESSE PICKY PERCH

The motion and flash of a small jigging spoon will get a perch's attention. If the fish is aggressive, it will hit the spoon right away. A less active fish, however, will watch the spoon but won't bite.

When finicky fish are giving you fits, try this rig. It catches these inactive perch and the aggressive ones at the same time, whether you're fishing open water or through the ice.

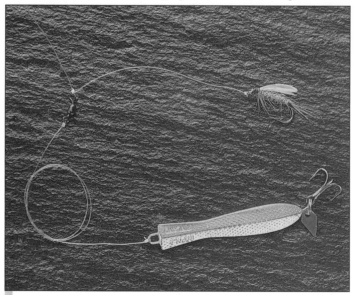

MAKE a tandem rig by tying a barrel swivel to the line. Add 8 inches of 6-pound mono and tie a small jigging spoon on the end. Attach 6 inches of 4-pound mono to the swivel; add a small wet fly or nymph. Even perch with a full belly are curious; they'll move in to inspect the flashy spoon and may take a nip at the fly.

DETECT LIGHT-BITERS

At times, crappies swim upward as they suck in a small jig, so you can't feel the strike. If you're using a regular bobber, it moves too little to notice. Here's a way to catch these fish, no matter how delicately they take your lure:

USE a European-style slip bobber (inset) on 2-pound-test mono to detect subtle takes. Tie on a 1/64- or 1/32-ounce jig. Add enough split-shot above the jig that only about 1/4 inch of the bobber sticks out of the water. Tiny European shot is best for the fine adjustment necessary. If a crappie swims upward as it sucks in the jig, taking some of the weight off the line, the super-sensitive bobber rises enough to clearly indicate a strike.

OUTWIT FUSSY CRAPPIES

In spring, you'll find crappies preparing to spawn in shallow water near cover such as brush or bulrushes. But often they don't feed much and shy away from most lures and baits.

Coax them into hitting by casting a lively minnow without a sinker. With no weight to hold it back, the minnow moves naturally and appeals even to the fussiest crappies.

NO-TANGLE TANDEM RIG

Popper-and-nymph combos are great for bluegills in shallow water. The popper attracts the fish, but most of them, particularly the big ones, hit the nymph.

One common way of rigging flies in tandem is to cut your leader and join the pieces with a blood or barrel knot, leaving a tag end long enough for the dropper. But tying a dropper this way is time consuming, and the flies often tangle. Also, you need to tie up a new leader or cut the dropper off to go back to fishing one fly.

Here's a rig that's quick and easy to assemble, doesn't tangle, and is easy to take apart when you want to use a single fly:

ATTACH a small cork- or foam-bodied popper to a 6-foot leader. Tie 2 feet of 4-pound mono to the bend of the popper hook with a clinch knot, then attach a size 12 weighted nymph. The popper makes a good strike indicator, disappearing when a fish takes the nymph.

A LITTLE LEECH LASTS LONGER

Sunfish will gobble up a small jig tipped with a piece of garden worm or nightcrawler. Trouble is, after one or two bites, the worm is gone. Here's a bait that's just as appealing but lasts much longer. Tip a 1/32-ounce jig with a 1/2-inch piece of a leech, preferably from the narrow head end, where the flesh is toughest. The bait is small enough to catch nibblers, yet it will stay on the hook indefinitely.

MODIFY JIGS FOR PAPERMOUTHS

If you hook a crappie in the thin membrane around
its mouth, the hook can tear out easily. Here's a way to
increase your chances of hooking a crappie in the tough
tissue in the roof of the mouth:

BEND the hook of a crappie jig about 10 degrees past its original
position. Now the hook is more likely to stick in the roof of the mouth
than in the membrane.

BRUSH BEATER CRAPPIE JIGS

Crappies often hang out in heavy brush and timber. No
matter how carefully you work a jig through the branches,
you snag up. Even if you don't lose the jig, you'll shake the
branches as you try to rip free, usually spooking the fish.

One solution would be to put a mono-loop weedguard on
your jig. Here's another way of rigging a snagfree crappie jig.

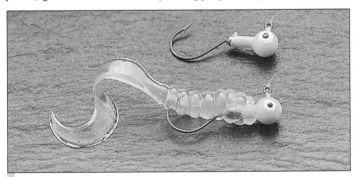

BEND the hook of a bare jig (top) downward about 20 degrees from
the normal position. THREAD on a plastic grub (bottom) so the hook
point is barely exposed.

PENNANTS FOR PANFISH

Catching spawning bluegills or yellow perch is easy because you can see them in the shallows. But once the fish move to deeper water, they can be hard to locate. Here's a way to bring the fish to you:

DROP a rope of colorful pennants (the kind car dealers use) in an area likely to hold bluegills or perch. A weight on one end of the pennants will keep them from drifting and a float on the other end will mark the spot. Leave the area for an hour or more. The bright flags attract these panfish and keep them in the area until you return. Fish around the flags with small jigs or live bait, either anchoring over the flags or casting from a short distance away.

READ DEPTH THROUGH BAD ICE

In early winter, you can easily sound through the ice with a depth finder. But later in winter, snow, slush and air bubbles interfere with the signal, so you have to drill a new hole each time you want to take a reading. Here's how you can sound through the ice, even if the lake is covered by slush and snow:

SOUND through recently drilled holes, where the ice is smooth and clear. Pour a little water on the ice, set the transducer in the puddle and take a reading.

SCOUT ICE-FISHING SPOTS IN SUMMER

Finding crappies under the ice is tough. You may have to drill dozens of holes before you get onto fish. And using a fish finder through the ice is far more time consuming than in open water.

When fishing in the spring and summer, find landmarks that will help you pinpoint your crappie spots once the ice forms. In early winter, the fish are found in the same shallow areas they occupy in the spring. By midwinter they move into the same deepwater spots they occupy in midsummer.

SUPER-TOUGH PERCH BAIT

The way yellow perch steal bait, you can spend more time baiting your hook than fishing. When you're jigging through the ice and fishing is hot, try this trick to make a bait that attracts perch with smell, taste and action and won't tear off the hook:

SCALE the belly of a small perch and cut out an inch-long strip. Split one end of the meat to form two tails. Hook the other end of the strip on the jig.

SEE LIGHT BITES
IN THE DARK

In midwinter, panfish sometimes mouth the bait so lightly you don't feel a thing. Or they grab the bait and swim up with it. Here's a way to detect these soft bites and set the hook.

Fish from a dark house or cover the windows of your fish house so you can see down the hole. In clear water, you'll be able to watch the fish take the bait. In deeper or murkier water, you probably won't be able to see the fish, but if you're using a light-colored bait, it will disappear when a fish grabs it.

PRESERVE PERCH EYES

Perch eyes make great bait for walleyes, saugers and even perch. So, when you clean a mess of perch, poke out the eyes with your thumb and save them. But don't put the eyes in a freezer or they'll get mushy. Instead, put them in

a small jar and fill it with salt water. Keep the jar in the refrigerator until your next ice- fishing trip. Use an eye to tip a lure, or thread one on a plain hook and fish it on a 4-inch dropper beneath a small jigging spoon.

CHUM FOR PANFISH

It's easier to bring panfish to you than for you to find them, especially when you're fishing through the ice. Borrow a tip from the saltwater angler's bag of tricks and try chumming. It works best for sunfish and perch, stirring up their competitive instincts so they feed more aggressively and keeping their interest so they stay around longer. Because fish must be able to see the chum from some distance away, chumming works best in clear water over a clean bottom, rather than in heavy cover. Here's how to do it:

DROP a few BB-sized chunks of frozen shrimp down the hole. Once the fish move in, chum sparingly but often to keep them around. As you change bait, use your old bait for chum. It's important to drop the chum in the same spot each time. When fishing in open water, drop the chum next to a marker or other stationary object.

LIGHT UP ICE-FISHING HOLES

When ice fishing at night, it's tough to see a bobber. Most anglers set a lantern on the ice, but the bobber may be hard to see because of the shadow cast by the rim of the hole. And when a fish pulls the bobber under, you can't see it at all. Try this trick to help you see better. It works with a light source as small as a candle or as large as a lantern.

Catfish Tips

KEEP BAITFISH ON A SHORT LEASH

Flathead catfish anglers often weight a big, frisky sunfish, sucker or bull-head with a slip-sinker and put a sinker stop about 18 inches above the hook so the bait can move freely. But in the tangled timber big flat-heads love, a baitfish on an 18-inch tether will hide in the wood or wrap your line around a snag.

Keep the baitfish close to the sinker by eliminating the sinker stop entirely or by placing a stop only a few inches up the line. Reel in the slack. If you want the bait-fish to swim a little more, feed a few inches of line through the sinker. With the baitfish on such a short leash, a catfish can catch it easily.

WILD BAITFISH TAME CATS

Veteran catfishermen know that baitfish caught from the river they're fishing are far superior to pond-reared baitfish purchased from the local bait shop.

Almost any kind of wild baitfish, including chubs, suckers and sunfish, will work.

The reason is simple: to baitfish that inhabit the river, catfish are natural enemies. When a hooked baitfish spots a cat, it struggles frantically to escape. The commotion arouses the cat's interest. A pond-reared baitfish, on the other hand, has never seen a catfish and has no reason to fear it.

LINE RELEASE FOR BANK FISHING

When bottom fishing from shore with live bait, you should keep the line under a little tension so the wind or current doesn't carry it out. Yet line must pay out when a fish bites or it will drop the bait. To get just the right amount of tension, try this trick:

SLIP a loop of line under a matchstick held to the foregrip with a rubber band. The match will keep the line from drifting away, but will release the line when a fish hits. If the current or wind is strong, increase the friction on the loop by pulling the line in tighter to the rubber band. If there is little current, or if you feel that light-biting catfish are dropping the bait because they feel resistance, move the line farther from the rubber band. This way, the slightest tug will pull it free.

KEEP CHICKEN LIVER ON THE HOOK

Chicken liver is a top channel cat bait, but liver won't stay on a hook if it gets warm and mushy. If you fish from the bank or a boat, keep the bait in a cooler. If you wade, pack the liver in a plastic bag and drop it in a canvas creel with an ice pack. Here are three other tricks that help keep the bait on the hook:

IMPALE the chicken liver on a number 8 or 10 treble hook (left), making sure each hook point pierces the bait. Whether the liver is firm or mushy, a treble hook holds it more securely than a single hook.

WRAP mushy liver in a patch of nylon mesh or stocking (middle). The mesh lets odors escape yet keeps the bait from falling apart. Form a bag, twisting the hook to close the top and hooking the mesh again to keep the bag from opening up. Or tie the bag shut with thread before pushing a hook through it.

MIX chicken liver with Wheaties in a blender to form a thick paste (right). Mold the bait into a ball around a bait-holder treble hook.

LONGER-LASTING SCENT

Catfish are drawn to some commercial and homemade scents, but many of these concoctions wash off after a few minutes in the water. Here's a way to make the scent last longer.

Cut a piece of sponge about 1-inch square and bury a bait hook in it. Soak the sponge in scent. Fish the sponge in one spot or drift it slowly along the bottom. Reapply scent every half hour or so.

The sponge stays on the hook well and releases the scent slowly. Because it has a soft texture like real food, a catfish will pick it up and swim off, giving you time to set the hook.

ENHANCE NATURAL ODOR

Flatheads, blues and big channel cats are lazy; they'll eat a good-sized baitfish but usually won't go much out of their way to do it. Here's how you can make any baitfish more appealing to big cats by slowing it down so they can catch it more easily, and at the same time increasing the amount of scent it gives off:

TRIM part of the tail and pectoral fins before rigging the bait with a slip-sinker. The smell of fluids that seep from the cuts will attract catfish. The bait will move frantically, but without normal fins won't be able to dodge a big cat.

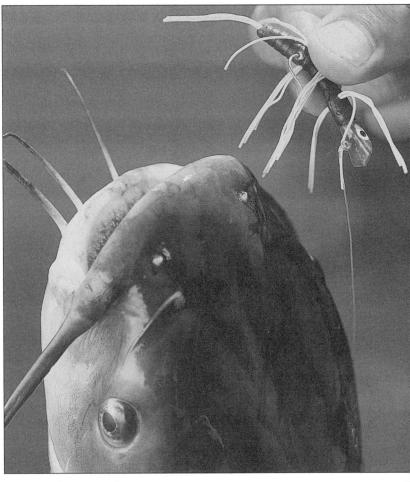

JIGS FOR CATS

Few anglers think of jigs as catfish lures, but jig fishermen who target walleyes or bass in catfish waters catch plenty of cats by accident. It's not hard to understand why jigs catch so many catfish: They can easily be fished on the bottom, right where the catfish are.

Jigs tipped with live bait such as minnows, nightcrawlers or leeches work best, although it's not unusual to catch catfish on plain bucktail, twister-tail or rubber-legged jigs. Work the lure along the bottom in slow hops, just as you would for walleyes or bass.

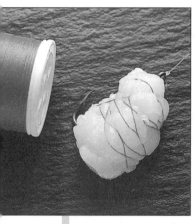

KEEP CLAM MEAT ON THE HOOK

Clams make good bait for catfish and many bottom-feeding saltwater fish, such as flounder and surfperch. The meat of a clam consists of the firm muscle mass, called the "foot," and some other tissue, which is softer. The foot is easy to keep on the hook; the other tissue is not. Most anglers use only the foot, but here's a way to make use of the soft meat as well:

WRAP the soft meat with about 8 inches of thread, leaving the hook point exposed. The thread will cut into the meat, making a knot unnecessary.

TOUGHEN UP BAIT

Almost any kind of dead minnows will catch channel cats, but dead bait softens up with use and tears off the hook. Here's a way to keep it on the hook much longer.

Spread the minnows on a screen and let them dry in the sun for several hours. The screen lets both sides dry out and toughen up. Use the minnows as soon as they're dry, or freeze them in a plastic bag to use later.

JUNKYARD SLIP-SINKERS

The debris-strewn bottoms of good catfish holes can gobble up a lot of sinkers. Here's how to cut your losses by making your own slip-sinkers out of otherwise worthless scrap:

TIE a heavy washer, bolt, nut or other scrap to a 12-inch piece of mono. Attach a barrel swivel to the other end. Slip the line from your rod through the free end of the swivel, and tie it to a second swivel. Run a short leader and bait hook off the second swivel. The "junkyard dropper" should be lighter than the main line. That way, if the scrap hangs up, the dropper will break, sparing the rest of the rig.

CATS WANT LEECHES — DEAD OR ALIVE

Most anglers think of leeches as good bait for walleyes, but leeches also work well for a lot of other species, including channel cats.

Walleyes seldom bite on dead leeches, but channels don't seem to care whether they're dead or alive. In fact, when cats are off the bite, the rank smell of the dead leeches often stirs their interest.

Save your dead leeches; you may want to use them in combination with live ones or with some other type of live bait. Dead leeches will keep for several days in cold water.

LIFT BAITS ABOVE SNAGS

Years after a reservoir fills, a tangle of roots, limbs and logs remains on the lake bed, making it difficult to reach bottom-hugging fish without snagging the debris on the bottom. Here's how some southern catfish anglers solve the problem. The technique will work in any snag-filled lake or slow-moving stream.

RAISE the bait off the bottom by pegging a 2- to 3-inch Styrofoam float about a foot up the leader (inset). The float lifts the hook and bait. The closer the float is to the hook, the higher the bait will ride.

FEEL YOUR WAY AROUND SNAGS

Big flatheads lie in deep holes filled with sunken timber. It's tough to know where to cast. Get too close to the wood, and the sinker or hook will hang up. Stay too far away, and the big cats won't find the bait. To place the bait properly, you need to figure out the precise location of the logs and limbs. Here's how:

FAN-CAST with a 1-ounce bell sinker tied to the end of your line. Retrieve it along the bottom. The sinker seldom hangs up, and you can feel it crawl over logs, limbs, brush and rocks. Once you get a clear picture of the bottom, you can cast near snags but not into them.

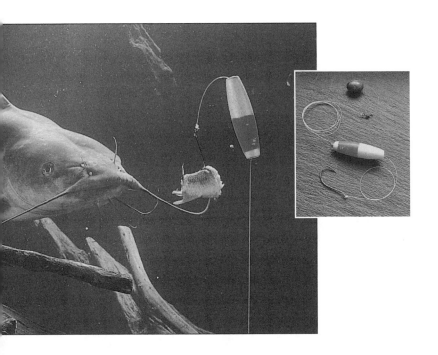

STEELHEADING FOR CATFISH

Most catfishermen add a good-sized sinker to their line and let their bait rest motionless on the bottom of the river. In time, a catfish will usually find it. But enterprising anglers have discovered a quicker way to get a cat's attention.

Remove the front treble from a crankbait and substitute a leader and hook baited with a minnow, a gob of worms, chicken liver or cut bait. Except that the baits are different, this is the same rig steelheaders use to fish along the bottom of a swift run.

Anchor below a riffle, or wade out into it, and let the rig trail in the deeper run downstream. You can move the bait from side to side simply by repositioning your rod. Reel in or let out line to move the bait farther upstream or downstream.

Even if the catfish are not in position to smell the bait, they can home in on the vibrations of the crankbait using their lateral line sense. Once they get close, they smell the bait and grab it, though occasionally a cat will hit the plug.

4

MAKING & MODIFYING
LURES

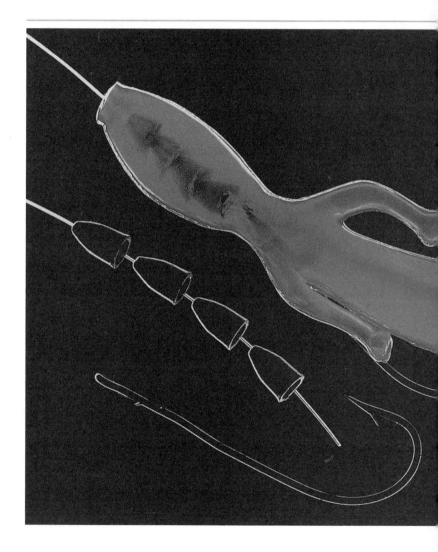

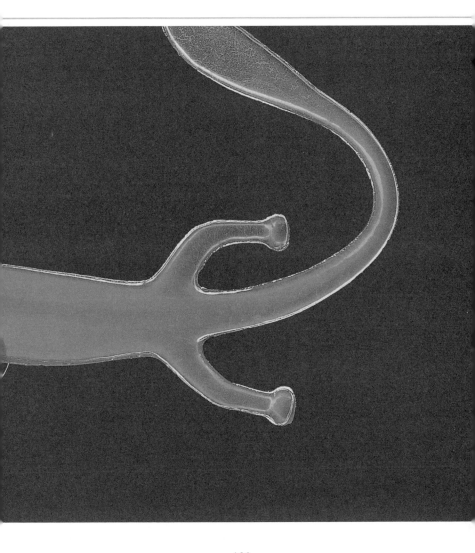

AN IMPROVED TEXAS RIG

With a regular Texas-rigged worm, you miss strikes because fish grab the worm behind the hook. But if you rig the plastic worm as shown below, the hook is far enough back to catch short-strikers. The sinkers are inside the worm, offering several other advantages:

They keep the worm from sliding down the shank when you set the hook; they won't separate from the worm, so pegging is unnecessary; and they're covered by soft plastic, so bass hang onto the worm longer. Here's how to make an improved Texas rig:

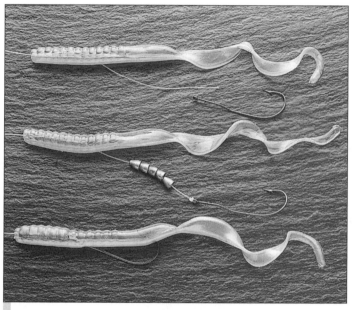

THREAD the line through a plastic worm (top) so it comes out about one-fourth of the way back. Simply use the hook as a needle. THREAD several 1/64- or 1/32-ounce bullet sinkers (middle) onto the line nose first and tie on the hook. DRAW the sinkers and the eye of the hook into the worm (bottom) by pulling on the line; push the hook into the worm so the point barely protrudes. The worm should hang straight so it doesn't twist your line.

SPINNING WORMS FOR BASS

Most plastic worm fishermen bump the lure slowly along the bottom. It's a deadly but very slow method. But when bass are scattered in the shallows, you can often catch more fish by using a faster retrieve to cover more water. Here are two ways to rig a worm so it can be worked rapidly across the surface. Because the worms are rigged crooked, they spin on the retrieve, drawing explosive strikes.

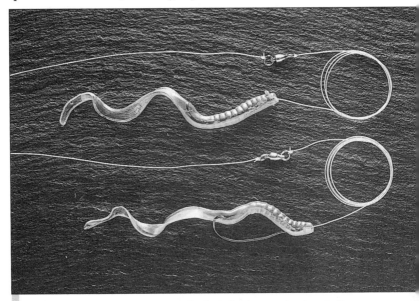

THREAD a 6-inch worm (top) on a barbed-shank worm hook so half the bend is covered. Add a swivel above the hook to prevent line twist. Slide the end of the worm over the hook eye; poke a piece of toothpick or mono through the eye to keep the worm in place. The worm has a kink in it so it spins when reeled in. MAKE a weedless version (bottom) by threading the worm on a worm hook and twisting it a quarter turn before reinserting the hook Texas style.

PLIABLE PEGS

Some anglers peg their worms by pushing a toothpick through the hook eye to keep the worm from sliding down the hook. But when you pull through weeds or set the hook on a short-striking fish, you may tear the worm off the toothpick. Here's how to keep the worm from ripping off as easily:

PEG the worm with a short piece of 80-pound mono; trim the ends flush with the worm. The mono has more give than a toothpick, so when you jerk, the mono bends instead of ripping through the worm.

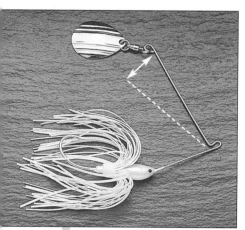

DEPTH CONTROL FOR SPINNERBAITS

How deep a spinnerbait runs depends on how fast you retrieve it. The slower you reel, the deeper it tracks.

But changing speeds to run at the right depth may reduce the number of strikes you get. Here's a way to change the running depth of a spinnerbait without altering the speed:

BEND the arm from its normal position to widen the angle and make the lure run shallower. To fish deeper, bend the arm the other way.

HARD-TO-THROW BUZZBAITS

Buzzbaits stir up plenty of action in heavy cover, but a leaping bass can easily throw the heavy, long-bodied lure. As the bass shakes its head, the lure flops back and forth, twisting the hook, enlarging the hole in the fish's mouth and allowing the hook to back out. But here's a way to doctor a buzzbait so it's considerably harder for a bass to throw:

MODIFY the buzzbait by snipping the shaft, forming eyes in the wire and joining them with a split ring. It's important to form the eyes by bending the wire up so the ends are behind the prop arm, where they won't catch weeds. The hook of this jointed buzzbait moves independently of the heavy blade, so bass have a hard time shaking it loose.

MOW WEEDS WITH A SPINNERBAIT

Thick submerged weeds, such as hydrilla and coontail, cling to a spinnerbait and ruin its action. Here's a clever way to modify a spinnerbait so you can work it through the weeds with fewer hang-ups. Select a spinnerbait with a heavy brass willowleaf blade and an attachment eye that is not twisted to form a loop in the wire. If the lure has a twisted eye, a clevis or beads, it will catch more weeds on the retrieve.

FILE the leading edges of the blade and hone them until they're razor sharp. Now, the blade will cut through the weeds so they can't foul the lure.

TUNING SPINNER BLADES

Commercial spinnerbaits and in-line spinners have cupped blades that start turning easily and spin rapidly. But sometimes fish don't respond to the vibrations of a standard blade. Here's a way to modify your spinner blades so they make a different sound, which may be more appealing:

FLATTEN the blade on a rock or anvil. The flat blade creates more resistance and a slower, more throbbing beat than the original.

TWO-WAY TRAILER

When spinnerbait anglers add a trailer hook to catch short-striking fish, they push it over the main hook point up (top).

This system works fine in heavy cover. The trailer doesn't snag many weeds because the hook point is protected.

But when you're working open water, try rigging the trailer point down (bottom). With one hook pointing up and the other pointing down, your hooking percentage will increase.

114

HOMEMADE TRAILER HOOKS

Many commercially made trailer hooks have vinyl-coated eyes to hold them firmly on the bend of the main hook. Otherwise, the trailer would flop around or fall off entirely.

If you can't find trailer hooks with vinyl-coated eyes, or if they're not available in the style or size you want, you can easily make your own using almost any long-shanked hook with a large straight eye. Here's how to do it:

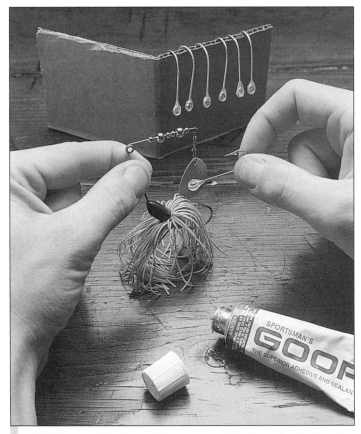

COAT the eye of the hook with a waterproof, flexible adhesive (the kind you would use to patch waders). Or, dip the eye in the liquid vinyl sold in hardware stores to coat and insulate tool handles. When the coating dries, push the trailer hook onto the main hook.

DOUBLE-SKIRTED SPINNERBAITS

Most spinnerbaits and buzzbaits have rubber skirts to add action, color and a full silhouette to the lure. Sometimes anglers want to add yet another skirt to make the lure appear larger, or to add another color or to slow the sink rate to keep the lure near the surface on the retrieve. But with a second skirt, bass may strike short. Here's how to add a skirt without reducing your hooking percentage:

MAKE a double-skirted spinnerbait by sliding a skirt over a trailer hook. Then push the main hook through the skirt's rubber sleeve and the eye of the trailer. Push the trailer into place on the bend of the main hook.

FIZZING FOR FISH

When fish are fussy, even the slow movement of a plastic worm or soft-plastic tube jig may not get them to strike. Here's an unusual presentation that can really pay off:

CRUMBLE an Alka-Seltzer tablet and slide the chunks in the rear of a soft-plastic tube jig. Stuff cotton in the tube to hold the Alka-Seltzer in place. Fish the lure slowly. As water soaks through the cotton, the Alka-Seltzer begins to fizz. The bubbles that stream from the rear of the jig attract fish and often trigger a strike. This is a proven tactic for largemouth bass, but don't hesitate to try it on other species, as well.

SNAG-RESISTANT SNAKE PLUGS

Fish can't resist the wild action of a jointed minnow plug. But it's almost impossible to use these lures in weedy or brushy cover because they foul immediately.

Here's a way to make a jointed minnow plug more weedless while adding the enticing swimming action of a plastic worm:

 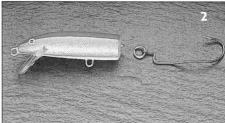

1. REMOVE the back end of a medium-sized jointed minnow plug by cutting or opening the rear eye; take off the front treble and split ring.

2. TWIST the eye on the front section so it is horizontal. Slide a split ring onto a 3/0 worm hook; then join the split ring to the plug so the hook rides point up.

3. RIG a 4-inch plastic worm on the hook Texas style. Fish the lure in pads, stumps and trees, retrieving it steadily so it swims at or near the surface like a snake. When a fish hits, pause a second before setting the hook.

MODIFY SPOONS FOR DIFFERENT SPEEDS

Lightweight trolling spoons have good action within a narrow range of speed. Troll too fast, and they spin, twisting your line; too slow, and they drag through the water without much wobble at all. You can find the best speed by trolling your spoon next to the boat and varying your speed until it wobbles just right. But a problem arises when you want to run that spoon with other lures that troll best at different speeds. Here's a way to make the spoon work at higher or lower speeds so you can use it with these other lures:

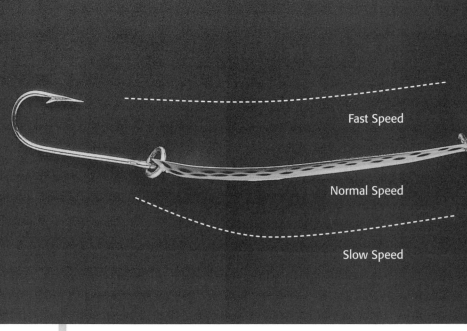

Fast Speed

Normal Speed

Slow Speed

TUNE the spoon for higher speeds by straightening it (top dotted line). Make it wobble more at lower speeds by increasing the bend (bottom dotted line). Bend the spoon by hand, being careful not to kink the metal.

HOOK BIG FISH BETTER

Most plugs, spoons and spinners come with treble hooks. But if you're after trophy-class fish, ordinary trebles may not be strong enough. Big-fish specialists know that a good-sized single hook will sink deeper and hold better than a treble, and no fish is likely to bend or break it.

If you're fishing in waters where there's a good chance of hooking something big, replace your trebles with single Siwash hooks. A Siwash has a sturdy shank and an extra-long slow-tapering point that penetrates like a needle. Once a fish is on, there's little chance it will get away.

Lures with a single Siwash hook offer another advantage: they can be used in waters where treble hooks are banned.

If the trebles are attached with split rings, you can simply open the ring, take off the treble and substitute the Siwash. If the ring is welded, you'll have to cut it off and add a new one. If a lure has two or three trebles, you may want to remove all of them and add just one Siwash where the rear treble was. Changing hooks may disrupt the lure's balance and ruin its action, so be sure to test it before fishing.

REMEMBERING THE RIGHT CRANKBAIT

Different crankbaits run at different depths. If you're fishing in 8 feet of water, you'll probably want a lure that runs 6 or 7 feet deep. If you can't recall how deep your crankbaits run, try this trick:

WRITE the running depth of each lure on the body or lip with an indelible marker so you know at a glance which crankbait to use. Running depths are often listed in catalogs or the instructions that come with the lures, but it's best to test them yourself. Different line weights and retrieve speeds will cause the lures to run at different depths.

FIXING THE WEAK LINK

You hook a big fish, it thrashes wildly, but then it's gone.

After you reel in, you find a hook is missing from your lure. A split ring broke, and the fish swam off with the hook.

This all-too-common problem can be prevented by soldering your split rings to keep them from pulling apart. Even if you have a soldering gun handy, however, you may have trouble getting the solder to stick.

Here's an easy way to beef up your split rings so they won't break at a critical moment:

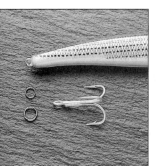 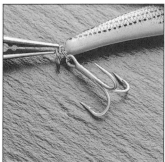 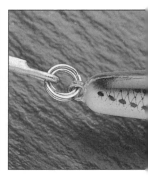

REMOVE the original split ring and treble hook (left). Find two split rings that will nestle together, so one fits snugly inside the other.

JOIN the hook and plug with the small ring first (middle). Start the large ring on the plug; then put it on the hook. A split-ring pliers makes the job easier.

FIT the small ring inside the larger one (right). Often, it will snap into place. Even if it doesn't fit snugly, the connection is strengthened.

EASY JIG EYES

Many anglers are convinced that eyes make lures more effective. But the eyes are tough to paint on neatly if you don't know how. Here's a way to do it right every time:

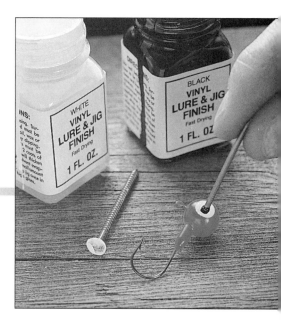

DIP the head of a large nail in light-colored paint and dab it on the lure to form the eye. Let it dry. Dip a finishing nail in dark paint to make the pupil.

QUICK PAINT STIRRER

Many of the paints you use on jigs, poppers and other lures are hard to mix by hard shaking when the bottles are full. And as the paint gets older and thicker, it gets even tougher to mix thoroughly. You could use a stick to stir the paint, but here's a method that's quicker and not as messy:

DROP a buckshot, small bullet (not the whole cartridge) or large split-shot into the bottle. As you shake the bottle, the pellet stirs up the paint.

FINDING THE LEAK

A leak in a hollow plastic plug will reduce the lure's buoyancy and may ruin its action. If a plug isn't running right, shake it while holding the hooks and split rings against the body so they don't rattle. If you hear water inside, you've found the problem. Here's how to find the leak and plug it:

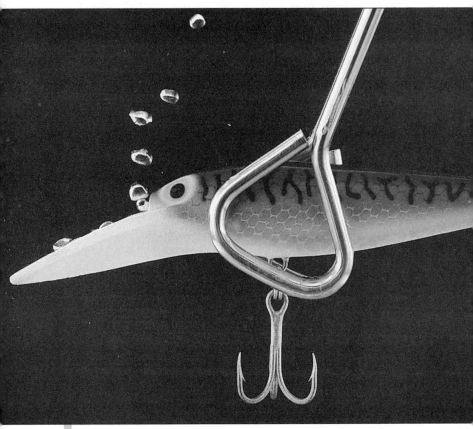

LOWER the lure, which has been frozen, into hot water. The rapid warming will cause the cold air in the lure to expand and bubble out of the leak, pinpointing its location. Shake out water if you can. If not, suck the water out through the leak or enlarge the hole with a hot pin. Patch the leak with epoxy.

HIGH-VIS DRY FLIES

Dry flies can be tough to see as it gets dark. And if you can't see a dry fly, it's tough to fish it. Here's a trick fly tiers can use to make dry flies that are visible, even in low light:

TIE in a tuft of fluorescent yellow or chartreuse steelhead yarn where the wing would be. Then wind the hackle "parachute" style around the base of the yarn rather than the hook. This method keeps the hackle from hiding the yarn, which will be easy to see, even at dusk. But trout will see the fly in silhouette and won't be spooked by the color.

BETTER SINKING FLIES

Most fly tiers wrap lead wire around the hook shank of streamers and nymphs to make them run deeper. But the lead wire causes the fly to sink horizontally. The water resistance against the entire length of the fly minimizes the sink rate. Also, the fly doesn't have much action. Here's a better way to weight flies.

Instead of wrapping lead on the hook, tie the fly on a bare jig. Flies tied on jig hooks have an appealing jigging action and sink head first, so they get down to the fish faster. Because they ride point up, they don't snag as often.

For best casting, use a jig no larger than 1/32 ounce. But jigs this size usually have hooks too small for good-sized fish. To get the hook you want, you can mold your own jigs. Or use bigger jigs and shave off some lead with a file or old knife. Another solution is to buy plain jig hooks (without the lead) and squeeze on a split-shot of the desired weight.

TOOTH-PROOF STREAMERS

Toothy gamefish cut ordinary tinsel-bodied streamers to shreds. Streamer bodies made by slipping woven Mylar tubing over the shank aren't very durable, either. If a few individual strands are cut, the body unravels.

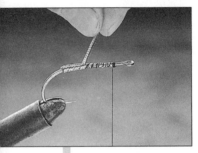

You can use that same Mylar tubing (with the string core removed) to make a much tougher streamer. Because the Mylar is wrapped on, the strands bind one another to the shank, so the fly won't fall apart, even if several are cut. Here's how to tie one of these durable streamer bodies:

MAKE a body by first putting a few wraps of thread around the shank. Lay the Mylar along the hook, wrap thread over it, then wrap the Mylar around the shank. Tie off the Mylar with thread. Continue tying the fly.

SNAG-RESISTANT WOOLY BUGGERS

The Wooly Bugger is one of the best flies for big trout and small-mouth bass. Most anglers fish it deep, with a splitshot next to the hook eye, so it moves up and down like a jig. Using a split-shot rather than tying the fly on a jig head allows you to change weight for varying circumstances. But the hook point rides down as often as up and frequently snags on rocks. Here's a way to correct the problem:

TIE the fly to the tippet with a Duncan loop. Hold the fly with the hook point up, and clamp a split-shot (BB or larger) to the lower strand of the loop. The weight keeps the point riding up so you'll snag less.

WEEDLESS POPPERS

Most fly rod poppers aren't weedless, so they hang up in the heavy cover where bass hide. Here's how you can make two types of weed-guards that will allow your popper to slip through weeds and brush.

MONO WEEDGUARD. Poke a pair of holes (top) on each side of the hook shank using a needle. Angle the holes out and back. Dip the ends of a piece of 30-pound-test mono in 5-minute epoxy, and insert them into the holes (bottom) to form a loop just large enough to protect the hook.

WIRE WEEDGUARD. Punch a needle (left) through the lip of the popper on either side of the hook eye to make a pair of holes. Bend a short length of stainless steel wire (about .010-inch diameter) so it has a tight loop in the middle. Push the legs of the wire down the holes (middle). Fit the loop over the hook eye (right), then pull the wire legs to tighten the loop. Trim the legs so they are just long enough to protect the hook point.

ENLIGHTENED FISHING

As the sun sinks below the horizon, a red-hot evening bite suddenly turns ice-cold. What happened? Is it possible the fish simply couldn't find your lure in the dark?

That may indeed be the case. When the sun goes down, light penetration may be reduced to the point where fish cannot see your bait. Lack of sufficient light is obviously a problem early or late in the day, but it may also be a problem in midday if it is overcast or windy; if the lake is covered by ice and snow; or if the water is deep or murky.

A study on an algae-clouded Michigan lake shows just how much murky water can reduce light penetration in both summer and winter (see chart on p. 127). In summer, for instance, 95 percent of the light was filtered out at depths of 8.53 feet. In winter, under snow and ice, 95 percent of the light was filtered out at a depth of 2.79 feet. With so little light available, even fish such as walleyes, with eyes adapted to darkness, stop biting because they can't see the lure.

But fishermen can beat the low-light problem by using lures that produce their own light. Some lures come with a glow-in-the-dark finish, but experts prefer to doctor their

own lures with luminescent tape or paint. The tape can be applied when you're fishing and is much easier to work with than paint. Be sure to use tape that is thin and flexible so it will mold to the shape of your lure.

USE flexible luminescent tape for easy application

DEPTHS AT WHICH LIGHT IS FILTERED OUT IN AN ALGAE-CLOUDED LAKE*		
PERCENTAGE OF LIGHT FILTERED OUT	**DEPTH (FEET)**	
	SUMMER	**WINTER**
20	1.97	0.66
40	3.94	0.82
60	4.92	0.98
80	6.23	1.64
90	7.87	1.90
95	8.53	2.79
100	16.07	no data

Based on July and February data from Wintergreen Lake in southwestern Michigan

If the lure glows too brightly, as many commercially made luminescent lures do, it will spook more fish than it will attract. Don't cover the whole lure with tape. A small spot or strip is enough to attract a fish's attention.

Don't flash luminescent lures with a camera strobe or Q-beam; it will make them glow too much. Instead, simply lift the lure from the water every 5 to 10 minutes to recharge it. At night, illuminate it occasionally with an flashlight.

Here are some ideas for doctoring your lures:

• Place one small luminescent spot or strip on each side of your lure to make it more visible in deep or murky water.

• If fish are right on the bottom, put a small piece of tape on the lure's belly so fish can easily spot the lure from below.

• Use a sinker with luminescent tape or paint ahead of a leech, worm or minnow. The glowing sinker leads fish to the bait.

• When trolling for salmon or trout, put a little tape on your dodger as well as your plugs and spoons.

• Add small dots or ovals of tape to spinner blades to make them more visible in dark water.

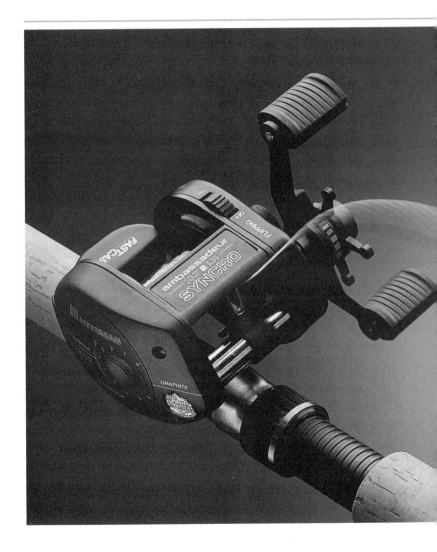

5

TACKLE
TIPS

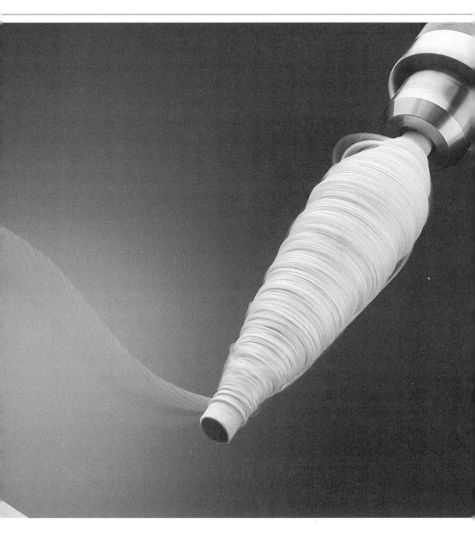

BUDGET LINE STRIPPER

Removing old line by hand is tedious. You can buy a line stripper to make the job easier. But either way, you end up with a tangled pile of line you can't reuse.

If you're stripping off expensive line, such as braided Dacron or lead-core, you'll probably want to save it. This makes the job even more time consuming because you have to wind the line onto another spool.

To remove line quickly and save it to use another time, put a 6- to 8-inch dowel in the chuck of an electric drill. Tie the line to the dowel, and run the drill at low to medium speed until all the line is removed. With a baitcasting reel, use the clicker or your thumb to keep the spool from overrunning and causing a backlash.

When the line is on the dowel, secure it this way:

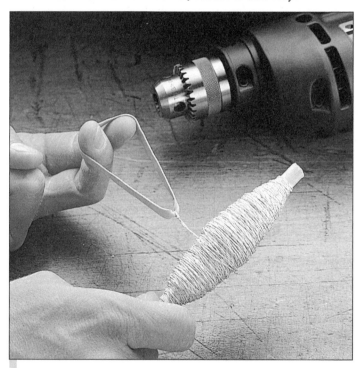

TIE the line to a rubber band, then put the rubber band around the dowel so the line doesn't unravel.

QUICK AND EASY LINE HOLDER

It's a good idea to carry extra spools of line. But spools lying loose in a tackle box take up a lot of space and are almost sure to tangle with your tackle. Here's an easy-to-build rack that will keep line in order and fit in a storage compartment in your boat.

Nail or screw together a three-sided rack from scrap lumber. Drill a 3/8-inch hole completely through one end piece and partly through the other. Slide a 3/8-inch dowel through the first hole and seat it in the opposite hole. Trim the dowel flush with the outside of the end piece.

Nail or screw a small metal flap to the end piece to cover the end of the dowel and keep it from sliding out. The flap pivots so you can remove the dowel.

Put a rubber band around each spool to keep line from unwinding. Slide the dowel through the spools, seat it and drop the flap. Keep a nail clipper handy by tying it to the rack with a short piece of fishing line.

TAME SPRINGY MONO

When first put on a spinning reel, heavy mono may spring from the spool as you open the bail, making casting difficult. You have the opposite problem with old line: it's so coiled it doesn't peel off the reel and pass through the guides smoothly. Here's a solution to both problems:

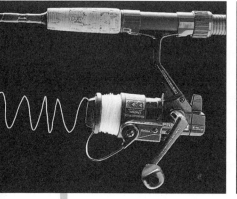 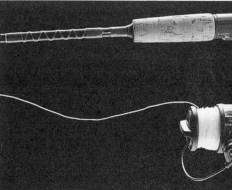

COILED mono (left) or line that springs off the reel can be softened by soaking your spool in warm tap water for about 10 minutes. WHEN you put the spool back on the reel (right), the line will be more manageable.

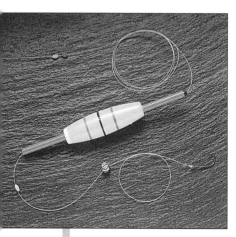

SAVE YOUR SLIP BOBBER

When slip-bobber fishing, your sinker may snag and you'll have to break the line. Without the sinker to stop it, the bobber will slide off, and you'll have to chase it. Try this to keep your bobber on the line:

TIE a slip-bobber rig as you normally would, with a bobber stop above the float. Then, add a second bobber stop below the float; it should ride just above the sinker. Now if you break off the sinker, the extra stop will keep the bobber from sliding off.

EASY PULL-OFF SINKER RIGS

If you're fishing a bait rig over a rocky bottom, it's a good idea to use a sinker that will pull off if the weight hangs up in rocks. That way, you just add a new sinker rather than make a whole new rig. But tying most pull-off sinker rigs takes time. The line, leader and dropper are usually attached to a three-way swivel, requiring three knots. Here are two simpler rigs that take less time to make:

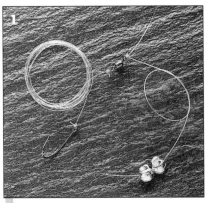 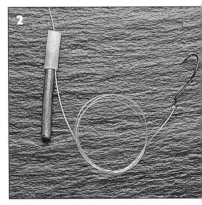

1. SPLIT-SHOT DROPPER. Tie the leader to a barrel swivel. Tie the line to the other eye, leaving a tag end several inches long for a couple of split-shot. This rig uses one less knot than a three-way swivel rig, yet it works the same way: if the sinkers hang up, a hard tug will pull them off the dropper, and you get the rest of your rig back.

2. PENCIL-LEAD DROPPER. Slide a 1-inch piece of surgical tubing over your line. Jam the lead about 1/4 inch into the tubing. Slide the tubing to the desired distance above your hook. If the lead snags bottom, a hard tug will pull it out of the sleeve. If it pulls out too easily, increase the friction by pushing it farther into the tubing.

THE CAT'S-PAW CONNECTION

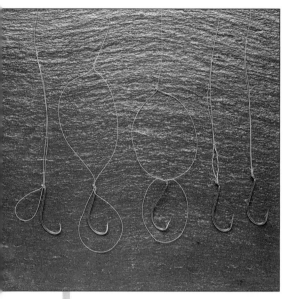

Double-strand leaders save lots of fish, but the way most anglers tie them, the hook will pull off if one strand breaks. Solve the problem with a "cat's-paw," a knot used by many saltwater anglers to attach a hook to a double-strand leader. The knot will hold the hook securely, even if a fish bites through one strand. Here's how to tie the cat's-paw:

TIE a 1-foot loop in your line with a strong knot, such as a double surgeon's loop (left to right), and thread the loop through the hook eye. Spread the loop and the two leader strands, and pass the hook through the loop and between the two leader strands, about five times. Start to tighten the knot by holding the hook while pulling with the standing line. Moisten the knot, then pull it snug. The finished knot resembles the pads of a cat's paw.

GETTING PIGS OFF JIGS

New pork chunks can be hard to get off hooks because the hole is too small to pass over the barb. Try this method to get the pig off your jig. Twist the pork chunk hard one way and then the other to enlarge the hole. Then stretch the hole over the barb and slide the pork off the hook.

STRAIGHTEN UP SNAPS AND SWIVELS

The right snap, swivel or hook is hard to find if you dump all your terminal tackle into one or two compartments of your tackle box. You can find these small items more easily if you sort them by size and string them on safety pins or paper clips.

BETTER SPRING-LOCK BOBBER

Many anglers like spring-lock bobbers because the long upper tip telegraphs light bites and is easy to see. But these floats have a couple of drawbacks: They are held on the line by a metal spring that may kink and weaken the monofilament. Also, pulling hard on a fish or snag can lift the spring, causing the bobber to pop off the line.

Here's an easy way to modify the float to solve these problems:

REPLACE the spring with a half-inch piece of surgical rubber tubing that fits snugly over the lower stem. Thread the line through the tubing, then push it into the notch in the stem. Slide the tubing up over the notch. Roll back the tubing to move the bobber. The soft rubber does not kink the line, and even the strongest pull won't cause the bobber to pop off.

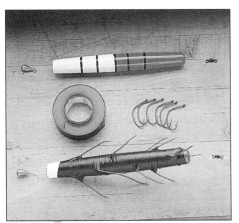

BOBBER GETTER

Large cylindrical slip-bobbers are popular with shore-bound catfish anglers. The floats are quite expensive, so it's painful to break your line on a snag and watch your float drift slowly from sight. Here's how some ingenious anglers recover their floats:

MAKE a "bobber getter" from a large cylinder float. Straighten a dozen large hooks, clip off the eyes, and shove the shanks into the float so the points angle toward one end. Wrap electrical tape around the float and the base of the spines to reinforce them. Run heavy mono through the float. Tie a barrel swivel to the end the hooks point toward and a 3/8-ounce sinker to the other end. The sinker provides casting weight and tips the float but won't sink it.

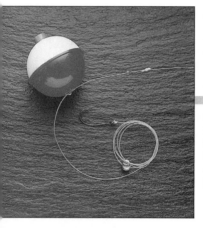

A CLIP-SLIP BOBBER

If you need a slip-bobber but have only a common round clip bobber (everybody has at least one), try this simple trick:

DEPRESS the button, pushing out the bottom clip. Turn the button to rotate the clip 180 degrees so it rests on the bobber rather than seating in the hole. Thread a bobber stop onto your line, add the hook and sinker, then clip on the bobber.

KEEP SKIRTS PLIABLE

The rubbery skirts on spinnerbaits, jigs and Hula Poppers tangle and get stiff as they age, losing their appealing action. Here's a way to keep them pliable:

SPRAY the skirts with Armor All Protectant, sold in auto stores to keep vinyl upholstery in good condition. Wipe off the excess with a cloth.

ORGANIZE YOUR WORM HOOKS

Rummaging through loose worm hooks is a hassle. And if your hooks aren't sorted by size and type, you can run short of the ones you need without knowing it. Here's how to keep your hooks in order:

BIND the hooks of each type and size together with a rubber band. You'll be able to find the proper bundle and slip a hook out in a moment.

NO-SLIP CRIMPS

To attach a swivel or other terminal tackle to braided wire line or downrigger cable, you can make a loop in the wire and crimp a metal sleeve over the wire and tag end. But if the crimp loosens, you lose tackle. Here's how to crimp wire so it won't pull out:

THREAD the wire (left) through the sleeve, through the swivel eye and back through the sleeve. PUSH the tag end (center) of the wire back through the sleeve. Pull the end to snug up the loop, but don't pull the loop into the sleeve. CRIMP the sleeve with a crimping tool (right); clip the tag end.

VEST-POCKET TACKLE BOX

Anglers who wade or hike in to fishing spots have to keep their gear compact as well as orderly. Here's one way to organize small items such as leaders, hooks and spinner blades when space is limited:

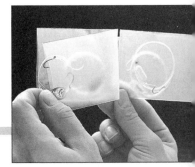

SLIP coiled leaders and other small, flat items into the sleeves of a credit card wallet.

LEADER TAMER

Tossed loose in your tackle box, pretied rigs such as leaders, worm harnesses and snelled hooks end up a hopeless mess. Here's one way to keep them from tangling while removing any kinks:

STRETCH out your pretied leaders after sinking the hooks in the edge of a piece of durable packing foam. Pin the loop of each leader to the foam, using an ordinary hook as a staple.

DO YOU GET THE POINT?

Everyone knows that sharp hooks are important, yet few anglers take time to sharpen their hooks. To make matters worse, they often buy the cheapest hooks, rather than spend a little extra to get good sharp ones.

The photos below depict just how dull some hooks really are and show the best ways to ensure that your hooks are sharp:

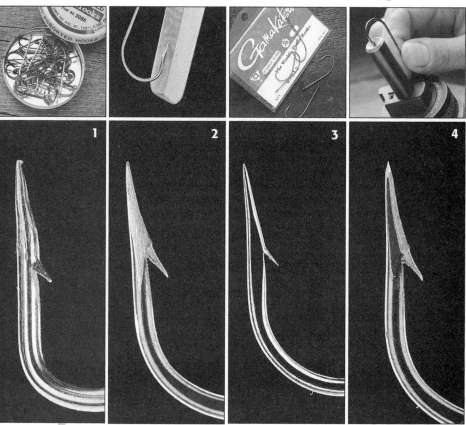

ORDINARY HOOKS (1) are surprisingly dull. You can (2) sharpen them to a triangular point with a file or hook hone. (3) Chemically sharpened hooks are even sharper than filed hooks, but they cost up to 10 times more. (4) A good motorized sharpener makes the keenest point of all, though they're a bit too bulky to carry if you fish on foot. One of the best is the Pointmatic Hook-Hone-R, which is easy to use and has long-lasting rechargeable batteries.

HANDY J-PLUG BOX

J-Plugs and similar conical trolling plugs with removable hook harnesses are popular for salmon, and many anglers carry dozens of them. To prevent tangling, some fishermen store the hooks and plug bodies separately. But the bodies take up a lot of space in a tackle box, and if you file them together in the same tray, you risk damaging the finish. Here's a neat way to protect the plugs' finish and keep them in order, making it easy to find the one you want:

MODIFY a tackle box by cutting a sheet of plastic, plywood or durable packing foam so it fits snugly in the box as shown. Drill rows of holes large enough to accommodate the plug bodies. Put the holder in place and set the plugs in the holes, head up. Store the hook harnesses in a separate container.

CONTROLLING LEADER COILS

Long wire and mono leaders are a nuisance to store. If you coil them and then wrap an end several times around the coils, it can be tough unwrapping the leader when you want to use it. Taping the coil is time consuming and difficult to undo. Here's an easier and faster way:

LOOP a thick rubber band around one side of the coil and cinch it up tight. No knot is necessary, so you can unwrap the leader in a hurry.

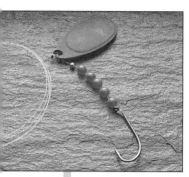

EASY-SPINNING SPINNERS

Most spinner-and-bait rigs have a series of beads between the hook and clevis. Sometimes, friction between the clevis and the last bead prevents the blade from turning freely, especially on a slow retrieve. Here's a simple modification that lets the blade spin more easily:

ADD *a very small bead between the clevis and the larger beads. The small bead has less surface area, reducing friction against the clevis.*

WATERPROOFING MAPS

Lake and river maps are always near water. If the maps you use while fishing aren't water resistant, protect them this way. Apply a waterproof sealant such as Thompson's Water Seal, designed for treating concrete block and wood. Spread the sealant on both sides of the map with a foam varnish brush. Cover the surface, but don't drench it. Use clothespins to hang the map from a line until it dries.

BETTER HOOK SETS WITH DIVING PLANES

Diving planes work well for deep trolling, but setting the hook may be a problem. Because of the water resistance of the planer, the full force of your hook set doesn't reach the fish. You can set the hook with considerably more force by rigging the diving plane the following way:

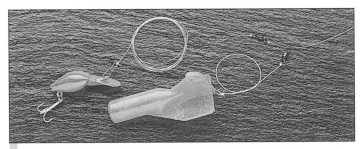

TIE about a foot of heavy monofilament and a barrel swivel to the front clip of a diving plane such as a Luhr Jensen Jet Planer. Run your line through the other end of the swivel and tie it to a second swivel, fastened to a leader and your lure. The diving plane will now slide along your line, much as a slip-sinker does. When a fish strikes, it pulls enough line through the swivel so you pull directly against the fish when you set the hook.

CONSERVE RUBBER STOPS

The small rubber stops you buy already threaded on a wire loop make handy sinker or bobber stops. Simply slip them from the wire loop onto the line and slide them into position. The rubber won't scuff your line the way other stops sometimes do.

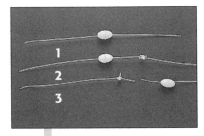

But the stops are fairly expensive, and once you take them off the line, they're difficult to put back on because the hole is too small to push the line through. You could rethread them with a sewing needle, but here's an easier way:

SAVE a rubber stop by (1) cutting it off along with a section of your old mono. To reuse the stop, (2) tie the piece of old mono to your new line. (3) Push the stop over the knot onto the new line, then cut off the knot. Slide the stop into the desired position.

LONG-DISTANCE BAITCASTING

Modern baitcasting reels are precision instruments, capable of casting long distances. But there are times when even longer casts are needed.

Shorefishermen, for instance, may have to make superlong casts to reach fish in midriver or to reach a drop-off in a lake.

If distance is important, you can modify an ordinary baitcasting reel to reduce friction against the spool, allowing you to cast a heavy lure or sinker 100 yards or even farther. Because the spool will spin much more freely, you'll have to thumb the reel more skillfully to avoid backlashes. Here's how to get extra distance from your reel:

1. CLEAN out the heavy grease in bearings, gears, the levelwind mechanism and other moving parts by spraying them with a light lubricant, which dissolves the grease and washes it away.

2. REMOVE the sleeves that rub against the spool and act as centrifugal brakes. If backlashes are a problem after removing the sleeves, replace one of them. On magnetic reels, remove the small magnets.

3. FILL the spool to increase its circumference. That way, the same number of revolutions of the spool will produce a longer cast. Small-diameter line also increases distance; use the lightest line practical for the water you're fishing.

BUDGET MARKER BUOYS

If you're moving from spot to spot or following a long break-line, it pays to carry a lot of marker buoys. Here's a way to make cheap buoys that are as good as the ones you can buy:

CUT an H-shaped piece from a thick sheet of tough packing foam. Tie one end of a 50-foot cord to the center of the H, then wind it on. Attach a 4- to 8-ounce sinker to the end of the cord. When you toss out the marker, the cord will unwind as the weight sinks. The marker's flattened shape will keep it from unwinding once the weight hits bottom. If the marker doesn't unwind, use a heavier sinker or cut down the height of the H.

KEEP COLD METAL UNDER WRAPS

One of the coldest things about fishing in chilly weather is the metal reel seat of a spinning rod. Here's how to keep the cold metal off your hands:

WRAP the reel seat with the tape sold in bike stores to cover handle-bars. Another option is the cloth self-adhesive tape that is sold in drug stores and resembles an Ace bandage. Either material insulates your hand from the cold and provides a comfortable grip on the reel seat.

BUNDLE RODS QUICKLY

When storing or transporting two-piece rods without a case, it's a good idea to bundle the easily damaged tip with the stiffer butt section. But putting rubber bands where you want them and getting them off again can be difficult. Here's a simple way to put a rubber band wherever there's a guide:

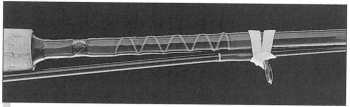

LOOP a rubber band over a guide, wrap it around the rod sections once or twice, and loop it over the guide again.

EASY HOOK KEEPER

A hook keeper near the rod butt comes in handy, yet many rods don't have one. Here's an easy way to make a hook keeper from materials you're likely to have on hand:

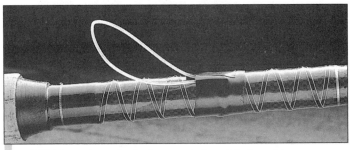

1. TAPE down the ends of a loop made from 5 inches of heavy mono. The loop should point toward the rod butt.

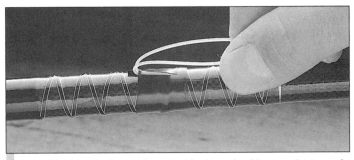

2. LAY the loop back over the tape. The loop should now point toward the rod tip.

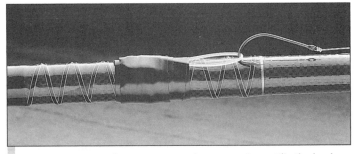

3. WRAP tape over the mono two or three more times. Slip the hook into the loop.

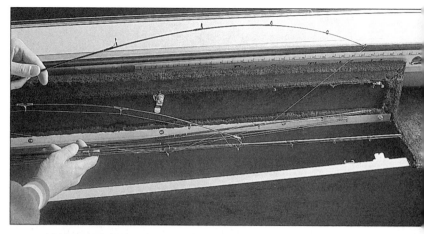

NO-TANGLE RODS

When you carry a bundle of strung-up rods in your boat or car, you invariably end up with a tangle of lines and

rod tips. Then, as you go to use a rod, you have to spend time unwrapping it from the other lines before you can fish.

Next time you carry a bunch of rods, try this method of rigging them before tossing them in your rod box or vehicle:

SECURE the hook on the reel, grab the line halfway up the rod, wrap it once or twice around the rod, and loop it over a guide. This way the line can't tangle.

CANE POLE LINE HOLDER

Two-piece cane poles and telescoping poles are usually rigged with a line about as long as the pole. When you collapse or un-joint the pole, you have extra line and nowhere to put it. Here's a solution.

Tape two paper clips to the rod near the butt. Space them about 3 feet apart with their opposite ends exposed. After you break down the rod, wrap the extra line between the clips.

CASE YOUR ROD AND REEL

A long fishing rod is a nuisance when you drive from one fishing spot to another. You can take off the reel and case the rod, which is time consuming. Or you can break the rod down and, leaving it strung up, toss it in the back seat or trunk, where it's likely to get broken. Here's a way you can safely stow a spinning, baitcasting or fly rod in a vehicle without having to unstring it and take off the reel:

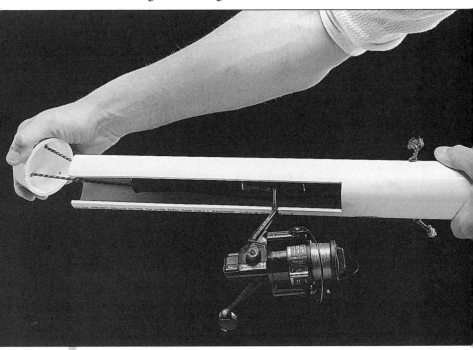

MAKE a case for a rod and reel by first cutting an inch-wide slot in a PVC or ABS pipe. The slot should be a bit longer than the distance from the rod butt to the reel seat. Drill a hole in each side of the pipe, about a foot from the end, and two more holes in a cap that fits the pipe. Thread elastic shock cord through the holes and knot the ends. The cord will keep the cap on snugly, but you can pull it off to put a rod in the tube. Glue a permanent cap on the other end.

FREEING JAMMED FERRULES

Graphite ferrules sometimes jam so tight that all the standard ways of freeing them, such as holding the rod behind your knees and pushing out with your legs to separate the joint, don't work. Trying to muscle the sections apart may break the rod. Here's how to get them apart without forcing them:

 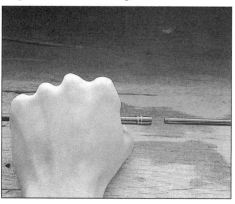

COOL the ferrule (left) by placing ice cubes on it or simply leaving the rod outside in cool weather. Both sections of the ferrule will contract.

GRASP the female ferrule (right) at the end. Hold it for 20 seconds; it will warm and expand before the male section does, so you can easily separate the two.

CORK CAULK

If your dog chews up the cork handle of your best fishing rod or a toothy fish takes a chunk out of a popper, don't worry. Here's an easy way to repair gouges in cork:

FILL the gouges with a paste made by mixing 5-minute epoxy and cork sawdust. Sand the filler flush with the cork after it hardens. Rod builders create a lifetime supply of cork sawdust when they turn down rod handles. Otherwise, get the sawdust you need by filing on a large cork.

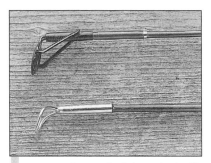

ICE-RESISTANT TIPTOP

Frozen tiptops plague ice fishermen. The ice clings to the guide struts, sharp metal edges and ceramic inserts and is hard to remove. Here's how to get rid of the ice easily:

REPLACE the standard tiptop (top) with a fly rod tiptop (bottom). It has a much smoother shape, no struts, and the thin wire has less surface area to collect ice. Any ice that forms is easily removed with your fingers.

NO-SLIP TIPTOP

Anglers commonly replace the broken or damaged tiptops on their rods by bonding them on with ferrule cement. They melt the cement, smear some on the rod, and put on the tiptop. But the tiptop strips off most of the cement as you push it on, so it soon comes loose. Here's how to install a tiptop that won't slip off or twist around on the rod.

Heat the old tiptop to melt the ferrule cement and pull it off with a pliers. Apply cement to the last 1/4 inch of the rod and install the new tiptop like this:

PUSH the new tiptop partway on and then heat it to draw the cement inside. Push the tiptop on the rest of the way and turn it so it aligns with the other guides.

WEAR-RESISTANT TIPTOP

Winter lake-trout anglers often use braided wire line for vertical jigging in very deep water. Wire line stretches less than mono or Dacron, making it much easier to detect strikes. But wire cuts through tiptops like a hacksaw. You could use a tiptop with a line roller, but it will ice up in cold weather. Here's how to make a tiptop that will stand up to wire line and won't freeze up:

1. FILL a brass tube 6 inches long and 3/16 inch in diameter with sand. Tape the ends closed to keep the sand from spilling out of the tube.

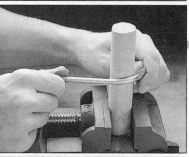

2. BEND the tube in a right angle around a 1-inch dowel or pipe. The sand will keep the tube from collapsing. Pour out the sand; smooth any rough edges.

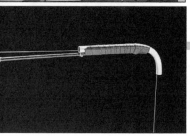

3. TAPE the tube to the end of a stiff 3- to 4-foot rod after removing the old tiptop. The tube lasts because it distributes wear over a large area.

BANK FISHERMAN'S STRIKE INDICATOR

When you're bank fishing with your rod propped on stick, a strong wind can buffet the tip. Other times, poor light can make it tough to see the rod tip move. Either way, a bite is hard to detect. You can tell when a fish is biting under these conditions by making a strike indicator.

One way is to clip the eye of a snap-swivel to a small clip bobber, and hang the snap on your line between the first and second guides. The bobber will rise as a fish takes the bait.

Trouble is, to reel in a fish, you must pull the bobber off the line, and that takes time. Then, if you're not careful, the bobber may fall in the water and you'll lose it. Here's a rig that solves those problems:

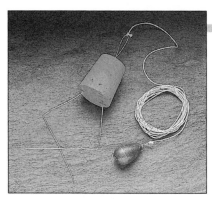

1. BEND 12 inches of stainless steel wire in half and twist a small loop in one end. Push the wire legs through a large cork as shown. Bend the legs outward and then back inward, so they cross and touch. The cork should be painted or wrapped with reflective or luminescent tape so it's more visible. Tie the cork to a 1/2-ounce sinker.

2. HANG the wire legs of the strike indicator on the line between the first and second guides. As a fish takes the bait, the strike indicator will rise. When a fish runs, line will slide through the wire legs. Jerk the cork off the line when you pick up the rod. The tether and sinker will keep it from blowing or drifting away.

SWIVEL GAFF

When you hook a big fish on your gaff and it starts
thrashing wildly, it can twist the handle out of your hand.
Here's how to keep a grip on the gaff:

*MAKE a swivel gaff by forming a hook from a sharpened metal rod
about 20 inches long and ¼ inch in diameter. Thread the last 2 inches
of the straight end. A machine shop can do the job. Cut a 1-inch hard-
wood dowel about 8 inches long for the handle, and drill a hole
through the middle large enough for the rod to turn easily inside.
Thread a nut on the rod, followed by a washer, the handle, another
washer and two nuts. Now, when a big fish thrashes, the gaff swivels
inside the handle, so the fish can't twist the gaff from your hand.*

TYING MULTISTRAND LEADERS

If you're tired of getting bit off by pike or pickerel, tie up a leader from small-diameter wire, such as 12- or 18-pound Sevenstrand. This twisted multistrand material doesn't kink as easily as solid wire, and it's thinner than nylon-coated wire. The problem comes in trying to fasten the leader to your lure, snap or swivel, because multistrand wire, unlike solid wire, is too springy to twist with your fingers.

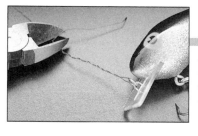

Here's an easy way to rig up one of these leaders:

1. RUN the wire through the eye of the lure or snap, leaving a 6-inch tag end, and clamp on a forceps.

2. SPIN the forceps around the main strand of the leader 10 to 15 times, keeping the wraps close together. The centrifugal force wraps the leader tightly.

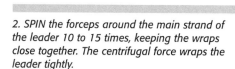

3. CLIP the tag end of the twisted wire close to the wraps. Attach a small barrel swivel to the other end of the leader in the same way.

ULTRALONG ULTRALIGHTS

Short ultralight spinning rods are ideal for fishing in tight, brushy cover. But longer ultralights are a better choice for most other circumstances. They have extra flex for casting light lures, cushion light line against the thrashing of a fish and give you better line control and stronger hook sets. Unfortunately, long ultralight rods are hard to find.

Build your own from a 3- to 5-weight graphite fly rod blank. Outfit the rod with the handle, reel seat and guides you would put on a standard spinning rod.

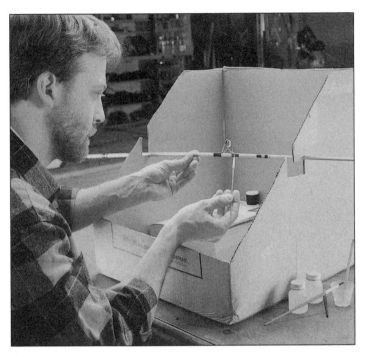

REPLACING ROD GUIDES

Rod guides wear out, they break, they loosen. Or, you may just want to replace your guides with better ones. A rod shop could do the job, but so can you.

First, you'll need something to hold the rod while you wrap the guides and apply the finish. You can make a good rod holder from a cardboard box by cutting the front and sides as shown. Cut a straight notch in one side of the box and an L-shaped notch in the other. This way, you can let go of the rod and the weight of the handle won't tip it. When you're done wrapping the rod, the box comes in handy for storing your tools and materials.

Remove the old guides by cutting off the rod windings with a razor blade or X-Acto knife. Be careful not to nick the rod blank. Remove any hardened epoxy by dampening a cloth with nail polish remover, acetone, or epoxy thinner, and holding the rag on the rod for a few moments. Then scrape away the old epoxy with your thumbnail. See page 155 to put on the new guides.

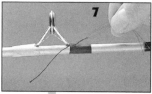
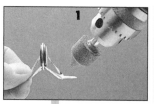
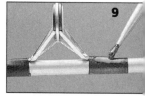

1. TAPER the top of the guide feet with a grinder so the thread wraps on smoothly. If the feet have blunt edges, there will be a gap in the thread at the end of each foot.

2. RUN the thread between the pages of a phone book or other heavy book to provide tension as you wrap the guide. The more pages on top of the thread, the greater the tension.

3. TAPE down one foot of the guide. Using D-weight nylon winding thread, start wrapping about $1/4$ inch beyond the tip of the other foot. Turn the rod to wrap the thread over itself.

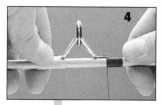
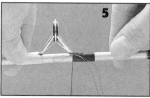

4. CONTINUE to turn the rod, making sure the thread wraps evenly without gaps or overlap. The thread will climb the guide foot smoothly. Trim the tag end of the thread.

5. LAY down a separate loop of thread when the wraps are about $1/16$ inch from the guide support. Continue wrapping to the support. Clip the thread several inches from the rod.

6. PUT the tag end of the thread through the loop. As you do this, make sure you hold the last few wraps with your thumb and forefinger so they don't loosen.

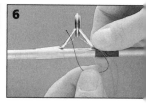

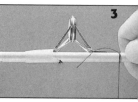

7. PULL the loop to draw the tag end underneath the wraps and out the side. Trim the excess thread. Wrap the other guide foot. Sight down the rod and align the guide.

8. REMOVE any gaps or overlap by gently rubbing across the thread with a smooth, blunt object, such as the barrel of a ballpoint pen.

9. APPLY rod-winding finish with a brush while turning the rod. Wait a day, trim rough spots with a razor, then add another coat.

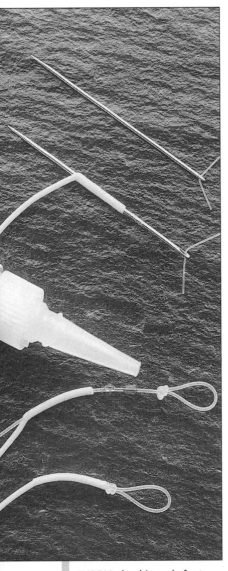

FIXING STICKY FERRULES

The graphite ferrules on some fishing rods often stick together. Pulling them apart is a hassle, and if you're not careful you may damage or break the rod. If you have a ferrule that sticks, try rubbing the male section with ordinary pencil lead. The thin film of graphite will lubricate the connection. After your next fishing trip, the rod should pull apart easily.

A BETTER NEEDLE KNOT

A needle knot is a popular way to connect a fly line and leader. But it's difficult to tie because you must slide heavy mono up the thin core of the fly line. The method shown below offers two advantages over an ordinary needle knot. First, it lets you slide heavy mono up the fly line core more easily. Second, you don't need a knot to join the line and leader, so the connection passes through the rod guides without a hitch. Here's how it's done:

THREAD the thin end of a tapered leader through the eye of a needle (top). SLIDE the needle up into the fly line core and out the side, about 1/2 to 1 inch from the end (upper middle). Pull the leader through until the pretied loop is within 1 inch of the fly line. COAT the leader between the fly line and loop with super glue (lower middle). PULL the loop snug against the fly line (bottom). Trim. Within seconds, the glue will bond the leader inside the line, forming a strong splice.

AIRLINE EMERGENCY KIT

You've shelled out a lot of money for an exotic fishing trip, but when you step off the airplane, your tackle is nowhere to be found. The stores available in many remote locations can't outfit you properly, so your vacation dreams are put on hold until the airline tracks down your fishing gear. In some cases, your tackle never arrives, and your fishing trip is ruined. Granted, the chances of losing your tackle in transit are small, but the result is often disastrous. Here's a way to guard against it.

Pack an emergency fishing kit and carry it on the airplane. Pack light because your baggage must fit under the seat or in the overhead luggage compartment. The kit should consist of a rod or two that can be broken down, reels, a spool of line and a selection of lures and terminal tackle. You may not be able to pack everything you want, but make sure you have enough to get by.

STRINGING UP A FLY ROD – THE RIGHT WAY

You rush to get on a trout stream during a big hatch. You're anxious. Time is slipping away. While stringing up your rod, you drop the fly line, which slips backwards through all the guides and lies in a coil near the reel. Now you have to do the job over again. Here's how to do it right:

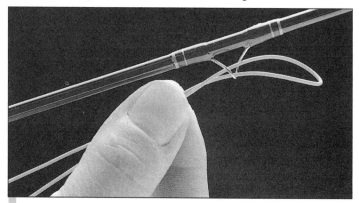

DOUBLE over the fly line or butt section of the leader and push the loop through each guide. Now, if you drop the line, the loop springs open and catches in the guide, so you won't have to start over.

STRIPPING OFF FLY LINE COATING

Some fly line knots and splices require you to strip several inches of vinyl coating off the line. You could use a wire stripper for the job, but it can nick and weaken the braided core. Or you could use nail polish remover to soften the coating, then strip it off with your thumbnail, but that's messy and inconvenient. Here's how to avoid these problems:

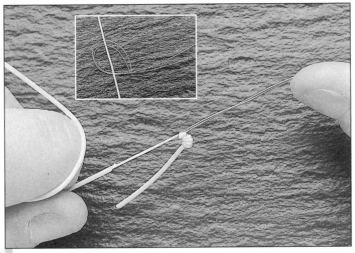

CINCH a loop of 20-pound monofilament onto the fly line, 2 to 3 inches from the end. With the doubled-up mono in one hand and the fly line in the other, pull hard and steady. The mono will cut into the coating and strip it off the core without damaging the core itself. If you have to remove a lot of the coating, strip it off 2 to 3 inches at a time.

PREVENT FLY ROD HANG-UPS

When a big salmon, trout or saltwater fish grabs your fly and makes a run, any knot or tangle in the fly line can hang up in the guides, popping one off or snapping the tippet. If you build your own rods, you can reduce the chances of this happening.

Use stripper guides, snake guides and a tiptop that are all a bit larger than you'd find on a commercially made rod built on the same blank. A knot in the line stands a better chance of clearing these larger guides without damage to the rod or tippet.

REPAIR DAMAGED FLY LINE

The vinyl coating on a fly line is surprisingly tough, but fly lines still get damaged. If a little of the coating gets scraped off, an otherwise perfect line is ruined. The damaged area isn't as stiff as the rest of the line is, so it "hinges" and causes troublesome tangles. The edges of the damaged vinyl hang up in the guides, cutting your casts

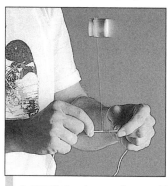

short. The exposed braided core is subject to abrasion that will weaken the line.

The coating is often damaged when it gets pinched between two metal surfaces, such as the seat and hull of an aluminum boat. If you do damage the line, here's a good way to repair it, saving an expensive line that still has plenty of life:

1. WRAP the damaged area with nylon thread or floss by twirling the spool around the line while holding the end of the thread under your thumb. A rubber band around the spool keeps the thread from unwinding.

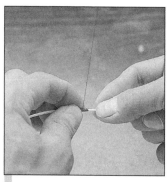

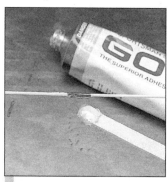

2. GUIDE the thread with your fingertips to cover the damaged area and about 1/8 inch on either side. Perfect wraps aren't needed. Finish the wraps using a loop of thread, just as in wrapping a rod guide (p. 155).

3. COAT the thread with a pliable waterproof adhesive, such as Pliobond or Goop. When the adhesive dries, the repaired area won't hinge and will shoot through the rod guides smoothly.

STRONG LINE-TO-LEADER LOOPS

The same wrapping technique used to repair a fly line lets
you make a strong loop in the end of the line for attaching
your leader. This kind of connection is more durable than
the common needle knot and you won't need a mono connector on your line. Here's how to make the loop:

STRIP (left to right) the coating off the last inch of fly line with a loop of
heavy mono. Fray the last 1/8 inch of the core to make a smoother
wrap. Double over the last 1 1/2 inches of line. Wrap thread tightly over
the exposed core and last 1/8 inch of the vinyl coating. Coat well with a
pliable, waterproof adhesive.

MANAGEABLE MARABOU

Fluffy marabou
streamers and jigs
look great in the
water. But in the
tackle box, the
marabou mats
down and picks
up rust stains from
other hooks. Here's
a way to keep the
flies in good shape:

CUT sections of plastic drinking straws a bit longer than the flies or
jigs. Cut a slot for the hook in each and slip the tubes over the flies.

DOUBLE-DUTY FLY RODS

Many anglers who wade streams are faced with a difficult choice as they begin to assemble their tackle: fly fishing or spinning? It's tough to carry and fish two rods, so you have to choose. Or do you?

Resolve the dilemma by using your fly rod for both fly fishing and spinning. A fly rod can easily double as a spinning rod. Its length is useful for drifting bait or small jigs, and it flexes enough to cast light lures. You'll be ready for anything, no matter what the fish are biting on. Here's how to rig it:

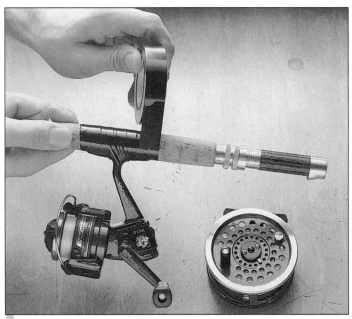

TAPE on the spinning reel when you want to spin fish, mounting the reel in the middle of the grip so it feels like a spinning outfit. If you build rods, you can make a straight cork handle without a reel seat and tape either reel wherever you want. Or you can install sliding rings to hold the reels in place. Outfit these combination rods with larger-than-normal guides so coils of mono can pass through with less resistance as you cast.

6

EQUIPMENT TIPS

NO-HANDS FLASHLIGHT

Night fishing can be frustrating. You can't see well enough to tie knots, untangle backlashes or unhook fish. Many of these jobs require two hands, so it's tough to hold a flashlight. But here's a way to see at night while keeping both hands free.

Strap a compact, battery-operated headlamp to your forehead. These lights, available in many sporting goods stores, are lightweight, and you can aim them simply by turning your head.

Headlamps also come in handy when gathering night-crawlers. You can carry your worm container in one hand while grabbing the crawlers with the other.

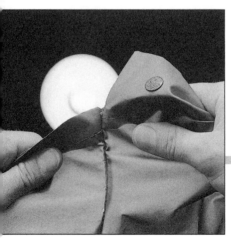

PINPOINT PINHOLES

Pinholes and leaky seams in rain gear are an all-too-common problem. You can patch most of these leaks with a waterproof sealer, but first you have to find them. Here's how:

TURN on a bright overhead light and hold the rain gear up to it. Spots of light reveal the location of leaks.

PERSONAL BUG DEFLECTORS

As you motor back toward the landing at dusk, you get pelted by insects. Unless you wear glasses, it's nearly impossible to keep the bugs out of your eyes. Here's an easy solution to your problem, if you have a cap with a mesh crown support:

PULL the mesh down so it covers your eyes. The mesh is porous enough to see through, yet fine enough to stop bugs.

REUSABLE HAND WARMERS

Chemical warmers keep hands and feet toasty in cold weather. They start heating as soon as you expose the contents to air. Though they produce heat for up to 12 hours, many outdoorsmen use them for only a couple hours and then throw them away, never realizing it's possible to stop the reaction and save the warmers for later. Here's how:

Seal the warmer in a small resealable plastic bag. The reaction requires oxygen, so it stops. As soon as you open the bag, the reaction starts up again.

BAG COLD FEET

Cold feet are a big problem for ice fishermen. Perspiration condenses in your boots, dampening socks and wool liners and reducing their insulating value. Here's a way to keep your socks and boot liners dry and your feet warm:

TRAP moisture by slipping a bread bag over a light wool sock before putting on a heavy sock. Then put on your boot. Your inner sock will get damp, but the bag will keep your heavy sock and boot liner dry, so your foot doesn't get cold.

WADER WICK

Once waders and hip boots get wet inside, they may take weeks to dry out. In the meantime, the cloth lining mildews or rots. And, of course, they're uncomfortable to use. Here's a way to dry them out quickly, and you don't even have to hang them up.

Fold down the tops as far as you can to expose the lining to the air. Then stuff loosely crumpled sheets of newspaper inside the boots. The paper wicks out moisture, which then evaporates. If the boots are very wet, replace the paper after a day.

SUBSTITUTE TRANSDUCER BRACKET

You may have trouble getting a suction cup bracket to stick on the transom of a rented or borrowed boat. Or you may break a permanently mounted transducer bracket while launching. Either way, you can't use the depth finder. But here's a solution.

Put the transducer in a small heavy-duty plastic bag filled with water. Seal the bag around the cord, then set the bag directly on the bottom of the boat (not on a false floor).

You can also set the transducer in the bilge without the bag, making sure there's enough water in the bottom of the boat to keep the face of the transducer wet. As long as there is no air space between the transducer and the water, the unit will read through the hull, though signal strength and reception will be reduced.

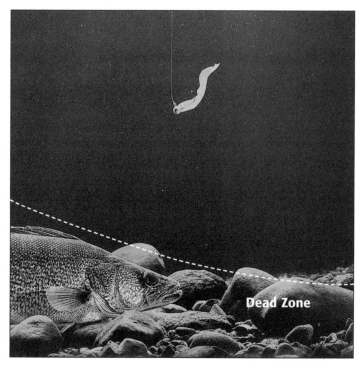

Dead Zone

UNDERSTAND YOUR BLIND SPOT

It's a mistake to fish only where you "see" fish with your graph, LCR or video. These devices detect bottom-hugging fish only if they're directly beneath the transducer. Elsewhere in the sound cone is a "blind spot" or "dead zone" just above the bottom. If fish are in this zone, you won't see them.

As the illustration shows, the dead zone is thickest at the edge of the cone and thinnest beneath the boat. The deeper the water and the wider the cone angle of your transducer, the thicker the blind spot will be.

You can't eliminate the blind spot, but you can gain a better understanding of what's happening beneath the boat by determining how thick the zone really is. Drop a jig to the bottom. Lower the rod tip to the water and reel in any slack. Lift the rod tip until the jig appears on your depth finder, and note the distance between the water and rod tip. That distance is the thickness of your blind spot in that particular part of the sound cone and depth of water.

GET BETTER READINGS THROUGH THE ICE

When using a depth finder for ice fishing, you won't be able to see your lure and the fish below your hole unless the transducer points straight down. But it's hard to aim the transducer simply by eyeballing it. Here's a trick to get it lined up right every time:

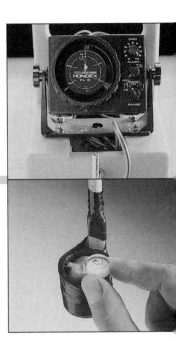

MOUNT a surface, or "bull's-eye," level on the top of the transducer with silicone caulk. Before the caulk dries, make sure that the transducer is pointing straight down by placing the depth finder on the edge of a table (top), aiming the transducer at a hard floor, and adjusting it until you get the most intense signal. THEN, with the transducer in the proper position, seat the level in the caulk (bottom) until the bubble is centered. When fishing, simply center the bubble to make sure the transducer is in the right position.

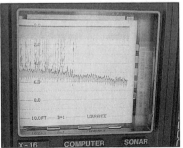

AVOID DEPTH FINDER INTERFERENCE

Some anglers run two or more depth finders simultaneously. But two units with transducers operating at similar frequencies will interfere with each other.

If you plan to use two depth finders at the same time, make sure they have transducers with operating frequencies separated by at least 50 kilohertz. A flasher with a 192-kHz transducer, for instance, will work fine with a 107-kHz LCR but a 192-kHz and 200-kHz unit are not compatible.

Here's how to recognize interference:

LOOK for scattered red bands that spin around the dial on a flasher (   ). Interference on a graph, LCR or video appears as clutter (bottom).

BIG "HOOKS" CAN BE MISLEADING

Many fishermen think a big hook on their paper graph, LCR or video means a big fish. It could be, but it could also mean a small fish. Here's why.

Suppose two fish of equal size swim underneath your stationary boat. The first fish is only a few feet down, where the cone is narrow. As a result, it passes through the cone quickly and makes only a short mark. The second fish swims near the bottom, where the cone is wide. It spends more time in the cone, and consequently makes a much longer mark.

Here's another example: You're drifting or slow-trolling and pass over a bluegill that is motionless or swimming slowly with the boat. It makes a long mark because it stays in the cone until the boat moves away. Then a good-sized bass swims rapidly through the cone. It makes a shorter mark because it passes through the cone more quickly.

Yet another possibility: You pass over two fish of identical size resting just off the bottom. The cone's edge passes over one, the center over the other. The fish in the center, where the cone is widest, stays in the cone longer and makes a bigger mark.

A more reliable indicator of fish size than arc length is arc thickness. The thickness depends on the strength of the reflected signal. And big fish reflect a much stronger signal than little fish.

PORTABLE "BOAT WINCH"

If you want to pull your boat up on shore and leave it for a while, you'll have to get it far enough out of the water that waves or wakes from passing boats can't pile over the transom. Pulling up a 12-footer is no problem, but a 16-footer is another story. Here's how to save your back. Lay two sections of 3-inch-diameter PVC pipe under your boat; roll the boat over them until it's high and dry.

MAKE YOUR ANCHOR BITE

When a strong wind blows, even a heavy anchor may drag across a sand or gravel bottom without digging in. A much heavier anchor might do the trick but would be a chore to use. Here's a way to make an ordinary anchor bite when you need it to:

1. LOOP a small second anchor onto the rope, about 6 feet above the main anchor.

2. TIGHTEN the rope. The small anchor won't slide on the rope, and you can easily take it off later.

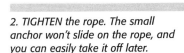

3. DROP both anchors. The small one will hold the rope down so the big one digs in. If you don't have a small anchor, use any heavy weight.

STAY DRY IN BIG WAVES

An anchored boat can be a wet place on a windy day, especially if your anchor rope is tethered to the highest point of your bow. The bow can't rise in big waves, so water splashes in.

The solution: Tie the anchor rope to the bow eye, which is closer to the waterline. If you have an anchor winch on the bow, clip the rope to the bow eye. Any spring-loaded clip will work. Even with the clip in place, you can let out and take in rope with your anchor winch.

Now, with the anchor rope attached near the waterline, the boat will be able to rise and fall with the waves rather than to plunge bow first into each one.

PORTABLE ANCHOR

Most anchors are too heavy to lug into hard-to-reach lakes. And it's often difficult to find a rock with the right shape to tie a rope around. Here's how to rig and use an anchor you can take anywhere:

LOWER a mesh onion bag filled with rounded rocks and tied to your anchor rope. If you're fishing over a rocky bottom, put one bag inside another for extra strength. You can make an even more durable anchor bag from a basketball net. Cinch the bottom shut by running a short length of rope through the netting, place rocks inside, and cinch the top with the anchor rope.

SNAGPROOF ANCHOR

If you fish over a bottom strewn with big rocks or manmade obstructions such as concrete slabs, you may hook your anchor so solidly you can't raise it. In fact, there may be nothing you can do but cut the rope. Here's how you can fish over rocky bottoms without losing your anchor:

USE an anchor with soft lead flukes. If the anchor hangs up, cinch off the rope and run the motor. The snagged fluke will straighten, and the anchor will pull free. Pound the fluke back into place with a hammer.

BARGAIN WADING STAFF

A wading staff is a handy but pricey tool for stream fishermen.

Here's a way to make your own wading staff from a bamboo or fiberglass cross-country ski pole, which you can buy at closeout prices at the end of the ski season. Ski poles are strong and have a point that digs in for a good grip. A loop on the other end keeps the pole fastened to your wrist in case you stumble and makes a good place to tie a lanyard for clipping to your vest or belt.

But the circular basket on most ski poles hangs up in brush. Here's a way to fix that problem:

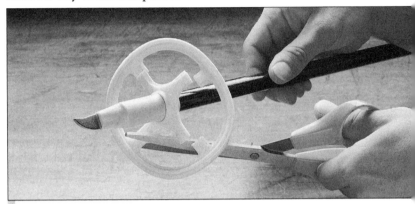

TRIM back the plastic basket at the bottom of the pole so only 1-inch stubs remain. They will keep the pole from sinking in a soft bottom but won't catch on brush as easily as the full basket does.

CUSHION GAS CANS

A gas can will vibrate as the motor runs, and its metal edges will scuff the boat floor. As you fish and move around in the boat, the can rocks against the floor and makes noise. Here's a way to protect the floor and keep the can quiet:

SLICE a piece of garden hose lengthwise and slide it over the metal rim on the bottom of the can.

CHEAPER PROPANE

Stoves and lanterns fueled by small propane cylinders are convenient for camping and fishing, but the cylinders are expensive and last only a few hours. Here's a way you can substantially reduce the cost of the propane and avoid frequent trips to the store to buy replacement cylinders:

REFILL a small cylinder from a large propane tank, using a brass coupler (left) designed for that purpose. PRESSURE from the large tank (right) forces the propane into the small tank with a hiss that sounds like air filling a tire. When the sound stops, the tank is full. Instructions come with the coupler; follow them for safety. By refilling cylinders, you pay only a tenth as much for the propane.

LONG-LASTING TRAILER LIGHTS

Leakage into trailer lights causes bulbs to burn out, and corrosion in the sockets ruins the fixtures. If you have to replace your factory trailer lights, try this:

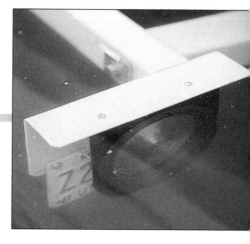

INSTALL sealed, waterproof lights. If you can't find those made for boat trailers, you can use taillights designed for tractor-trailer rigs. Sealed lights are a little more expensive than non-waterproof lights, but they last much longer.

CHEAP "POWER-TRIM"

If your motor doesn't have power-trim or a shallow-water tilt mechanism, you've got a problem when running in shallow water. Here's a way to prevent grinding your prop into the bottom:

RAISE the outboard by hand, then lay a 2 x 2, an ax handle or a piece of closet pole between the motor and the bracket that attaches it to the transom. Be sure the wood doesn't rest against and damage the reverse lock mechanism, a latch that prevents the motor from tilting up when you run it in reverse or neutral.

DON'T TIRE WHILE TUBING

In a float tube, you can maintain your position in a breeze by kicking your feet, leaving your hands free to fish. But a stiff breeze can wear you out. And if you let yourself drift, it may be a long way back to your put-in point. Here's a simple way of holding your position when you get tired of kicking:

LOWER an anchor tied to a stout cord. Any weight will do, but a couple pounds is all that's needed to hold a tube in a light wind. Tie the other end of the cord to the tube. Wrap the extra cord on a marker buoy or chunk of packing foam to keep it from tangling. When you drop anchor, simply half-hitch the line around the buoy and put it in a pocket of the tube. The anchor also lets you maintain your position over fish. Otherwise, it's easy to lose your bearings and drift away, even on a calm day.

EASY TIE-DOWN FOR CARTOP LOADS

When carrying a canoe or small boat on a car, it's important to use a knot that can be tied and untied easily but holds the load securely. Many people throw the rope over the boat, tie a loop in the rope, run it under the rack and back through the loop, then pull the rope tight and tie it off. But when you want to use the rope again, you have a loop in it that's too tight to untie. Here's how to tie a knot, called the trucker's hitch, that gets the job done but won't leave a permanent loop in your rope:

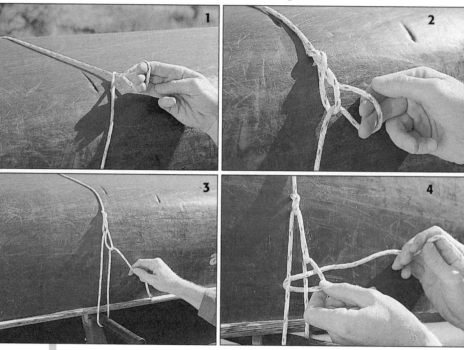

1. FORM a loop with two twists about a foot above the roof rack by slipping your fingers under the rope and rotating your wrist twice.

2. DRAW the lower strand of the rope through the original loop, forming a second loop as shown. Pull the second loop tight.

3. RUN the free end of the rope around the rack and then through the loop. Pull on the free end to tighten the rope over the load.

4. WRAP the free end around both strands of rope and tie a half-hitch, pulling it snug against the loop. Finish with a second half-hitch.

THE LOWDOWN ON MOTOR HEIGHT

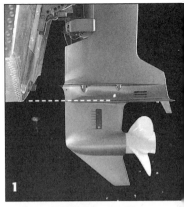

To get the best performance from your outboard, it must be set to the right height. If the shaft extends too far into the water, the extra drag reduces your speed, increases fuel consumption and sprays water.

If the motor is too high, the hull interferes with the flow of water to the prop, causing it to over-rev and lose thrust. Here's how to determine if your motor is set to the proper height and what to do if it isn't:

1. CHECK the height of the outboard's cavitation plate; it should be at about the same height as the bottom of the hull.

2. ELEVATE the motor if it's too low. Set a board on the transom as shown before putting on the motor and tightening the bracket. To elevate a motor that is bolted on, remove the bolts and reinsert them through holes lower in the bracket. If the motor is too high, lower it by reinserting the bolts in holes higher in the bracket; you may have to notch the transom to lower the motor.

COLD-CLIMATE BOAT STORAGE

If you store your boat in a cold climate, don't keep it in a level position. Water can puddle between the ribs and hull, inside gunwales, and in other small spaces, loosening or breaking parts of the boat as it freezes and expands. Even aluminum and fiberglass, materials normally considered weatherproof, can be damaged this way.

You can solve the problem by storing the boat with the bow raised slightly so water drains away. If you keep the boat right side up, remove the drain plug. Even if the boat is kept outside and exposed to rain and freezing temperatures, most water will run out before it can turn to ice.

CANOE ROD HOLDERS

Most canoes have no good place to lay a fishing rod. If you set them in the bottom, they slide to the center, where they can get broken. Here's a good way to keep rods where they're handy but out of the way:

SLIP the tip and handle of each rod into 2-inch-diameter pipe couplings attached to the cross members and seats of the canoe with 6-inch-long nylon wire ties, available in hardware stores.

WALK THE PLANK

When launching a boat from a trailer with bunks, you may have to walk partway down the trailer frame to push the boat off. And to get it back on the trailer, you may have to walk on the frame once again, often in the dark. Trying to keep your balance is nearly impossible. Eventually you'll slip off and fall in the water and perhaps get seriously hurt. Here's something you can do to keep your footing:

STAND on a 1-by-8-inch plank that you've bolted to the trailer frame, while launching and loading your boat. Apply non-skid tape to the plank, or paint it and sprinkle on sand before the paint dries to create a rough surface.

LAUNCHING WITHOUT A RAMP

Occasionally you may want to launch your boat where there's no concrete ramp or where low water has left several feet of soft sand between the ramp and the lake or river. If you try to back the boat in with your vehicle, you may get stuck. Here's a way to launch your boat under these difficult circumstances:

1. TIE a strong rope from your trailer tongue to your hitch (left) while the vehicle is parked on solid ground. Lower the tongue jack, if there is one. Then unhook the trailer, making sure it doesn't get away from you.

2. ROLL the trailer and boat down to the water (right). In soft sand, you may have to push a bit. The rope should be short enough to keep the trailer from rolling all the way into the water. As you launch, stand on the trailer tongue for counterweight.

3. HAUL the trailer slowly to solid ground while lifting the tongue enough to keep it from digging in. Don't attempt to roll the trailer out on the tongue jack, because the jack may catch on the ground and bend or break.

4. LOAD the boat after rolling the trailer back into the water with the rope attached. As you crank, you must stand on the trailer tongue to keep it from lifting. Hold the tongue up as the vehicle pulls the boat out.

Battery Tips

CHARGE TWO BATTERIES AT A TIME

You come in after a day's fishing with two drained batteries and want to head out again first thing in the morning. How can you charge both with only one battery charger? You could charge one battery at a time, but you'd have to get up in the middle of the night to switch the cables. Instead, try this trick.

Connect the batteries in parallel (positive-to-positive, negative-to-negative) with 10-gauge or heavier cable. Hook the charger to one of the batteries. Use a trickle charger (also known as a taper-type), which includes most marine and automotive chargers. These gradually reduce the amount of current as the batteries approach full charge.

Multiple batteries take longer to charge than a single one. Two fully discharged batteries, for example, take about twice as long as a single fully discharged battery of equal size. For that reason, you'll need at least a 20-amp charger to do the job overnight. To make sure both batteries are fully charged, check each with a battery gauge or voltmeter.

Charging in parallel works even if batteries have been discharged to different levels. But if the difference is great, one battery reaches full charge long before the other and may overcharge while the other is still charging. In this situation, it's best to charge the batteries separately.

BATTERY SAFETY

Batteries are filled with corrosive chemicals and produce explosive gases when charging. For these reasons, they are hazardous if used or charged improperly. Take these precautions to avoid trouble:

• Don't check the battery's charge, as some people do, by laying a wrench or other heavy piece of metal between the posts to make a spark. That test tells you little about the charge level. But the surge of current through the wrench from a fully charged battery can melt lead posts in a fraction of a second, as the sparks can ignite accumulated hydrogen and oxygen, causing an explosion.

• To avoid sparks, connect the charger to the battery posts before plugging it in. When finished, unplug the charger before unhooking the leads. If the posts are dirty, they'll spark when you try to make the connection. Clean them with a wire brush first.

• Keep the vent caps on a standard battery when charging it. The caps are designed so that flames from igniting gas can't follow back into the battery.

• If you spill battery acid, sprinkle on an equal volume of baking soda to neutralize it. Then add water to form a slurry, which you can clean up. Wear glasses and rubber gloves to protect eyes and hands.

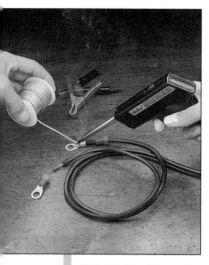

AVOID ALLIGATORS

Some electric trolling motors come equipped with alligator clips that connect to the battery terminals. The clips are quick and convenient. But with little surface area touching the terminals, alligator clips make a poor connection, causing a drop in voltage. To compensate, the trolling motor draws more current, draining the battery more quickly.

Here's how to improve the connection and get more running time out of your battery:

REPLACE the alligator clips with connectors, such as those shown, that can be attached snugly to the battery terminal with wing nuts. Connectors of this type provide plenty of surface area for the current to flow across. Crimp and then solder the connectors for the best conductivity. When installing any connector, be careful not to cut individual strands in the cable as you strip insulation. Losing even a few reduces conductivity and drains the battery faster.

STORING A BATTERY

If you store a boat battery improperly during the off-season, you may shorten its life or reduce its capacity. These tips will keep a battery in good shape.

Disconnect the battery. Charge it fully and store it in a cool, dry place. Outside is fine, but be sure to keep it fully charged. Don't store a battery in a warm place; higher temperatures speed up the self-discharge reaction that causes lead sulfate crystals to form on the plates, ruining the battery.

Contrary to popular belief, modern batteries can be stored on a cement floor without discharging.

Check the charge level every two months; never let it fall below 75 percent charge (12.4 volts). Subzero temperatures can freeze a discharged battery, almost always ruining it.

EXTEND BATTERY LIFE

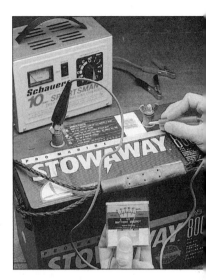

Many anglers charge their marine batteries with automatic battery chargers designed for automobiles. To provide a margin of safety against overcharging, many units shut off before they deliver a full charge. As a result, the battery discharges before it should. More important, repeated undercharging allows lead sulfate crystals to build up on the plates, reducing the battery's capacity and shortening its life. Here's how to tell if you're getting a full charge on your battery.

Charge the battery as usual. Wait 24 hours or turn on the boat's running lights for five minutes to get rid of "gas voltage" that causes a deceptively high reading right after charging. Then use a battery gauge (shown) to measure charge level. If you don't have a battery gauge, use a voltmeter and the table below.

If your automatic charger isn't fully charging your battery, use one with a timer or manual shut-off. By knowing the charge level, battery capacity and charger output, you can use the information that came with your battery to calculate how long to leave the battery on your manual charger. Charging too long corrodes the plates, shortening battery life.

HOW TO DETERMINE CHARGE LEVEL FROM VOLTAGE*	
12.6 volts	100% charged
12.4	75%
12.2	50%
12	25%
11.9	Discharged

Some batteries may reach full charge at a slightly higher voltage. Consult battery label, instructions or manufacturer for details.

7
AFTER
THE CATCH

Mounting Preparation

IN remote country, tether your fish in deep water to keep it alive.

You've just brought the fish of a lifetime to boatside. This is the one you want for the wall. Be sure the things you do from here on out keep the fish in good condition so it will look as realistic on the wall as it does in the water.

If possible, land trophy muskies, pike, lake trout and other big fish with a cradle (photo at left), by hand, by carefully gaffing them in the mouth or by beaching them. A landing net will knock off scales and split the tail and fns. Repairing is difficult.

Fish begin to decompose shortly after death, so freeze them as soon as you can. On trips where no freezer is available, keep the fish alive until you are ready to leave. Tether it on a 30-foot nylon cord tied to its lower jaw. Attach the cord along a steep shoreline where the bottom is free of snags; this way, the fish can rest in deep, cool water.

Take a color photograph of the fish while it is still alive. A photo will help your taxidermist restore the fish to its original color. Kill the fish by whacking it on the head with a blunt object. Don't use anything that would cut the skin or remove scales. Don't remove the entrails or gills. Sprinkle powdered borax or a commercial color preservative on the fish's skin.

Wrap the fish in a wet towel, binding the fins tightly against the body to protect them. Don't fan the tail; doing so makes it easier to damage. Don't wrap the fish in newspaper; the ink discolors the skin.

Put the fish, still wrapped in the towel, in a large plastic bag. Squeeze out the air, wrap the bag with tape, then freeze. Label the bag with your name, address, fishing license number, and date the fish was caught. This information will aid any conservation officer that checks your catch. It will also help your taxidermist identify the fish as yours.

If possible, store the fish in a chest freezer, which keeps items colder than freezer-refrigerator combinations. Avoid frost-free freezers, which rely on a small fan to circulate air to prevent frost build-up. The circulation can dry out the fish and contribute to freezer burn.

If a mount you admire was done by a taxidermy company, get the name of the person who did the work. Some companies employ many taxidermists, and all are not equally skilled.

When finding a place on your wall for your trophy, avoid heat and humidity. A fish may look great over the fireplace, but the heat will dry it out. Also, direct sunlight will cause the fish to fade.

Dust your mount occasionally with a featherduster or a soft cloth dampened with water. Gently stroke the fish from the head toward the tail to avoid damaging any of the scales.

More and more anglers release their trophies and buy "museum mounts," which are fiberglass or carbon-fiber replicas of their catches. To get the best likeness of your fish, carefully measure its length and girth. Weigh it if you have a scale. Finally, take a color photo to help match the model to the original.

Quick and Easy Shore Lunches

One of the best meals going is a mess of fish cooked over an open fire on the bank of a lake or stream. The scenery is terrific, and the fish is guaranteed fresh.

But preparing a shore lunch takes up a lot of fishing time, so you'll want something simple and fast. The recipes that follow require little time for preparation or cleanup, yet they taste great. Many of the ingredients can be prepared at home and put in sealable plastic containers or parceled out and wrapped in the foil you'll use for cooking.

Most any kind of fish can be used with these recipes. You can cook on a grate, directly on the coals or on a camp stove.

One of the biggest problems when cooking in foil over an open fire is telling when the food is done, because cooking time varies with the type of wood, wind, and outside temperature. With any of these recipes, simply open the foil and test the food with a fork. The fish should flake easily, and the vegetables should be tender. If the food is not done, reseal the package and put it back on the fire.

Here's how to prepare four tasty shore lunches:

SEASONED FISH AND VEGETABLES

Place a medium-sized fillet on an 18-by-18-inch piece of heavy-duty aluminum foil. Sprinkle the fish with 1/8 teaspoon salt, 1/8 teaspoon pepper and 1/2 teaspoon dried basil leaves. Top the fish with one thinly sliced (1/4-inch thick) medium-sized potato, two thinly sliced carrots, one onion sliced and separated into rings, and 1 tablespoon butter. Sprinkle salt and pepper on the vegetables.

Wrap and seal the foil. Place the fish on the grate and cook for 15 to 20 minutes.

FILLETS WITH BACON, MAYO AND ONION

Form a shallow tray with an 18-by-18-inch piece of heavy-duty aluminum wrap. Place several pats of butter and thin slices of onion on the foil. Lay a medium-sized fillet on the onions. Spread real mayonnaise on the fillet, and season with salt and pepper. Top the fish with bacon strips and grated sharp cheddar.

Seal the aluminum foil; cook the packet for 15 to 20 minutes. Open the foil to check the bacon. When it's done, so is the fish.

BACON-BAKED FISH AND PEPPER STRIPS

Lay a medium-sized fillet on an 18-by-18-inch piece of foil. Top it with a small green pepper cut into strips, a small onion sliced and separated into rings, and two slices of bacon cut into I-inch pieces. Salt and pepper to taste. Wrap and seal the aluminum foil, and cook the fish 15 to 20 minutes. Then open the foil to see if the bacon is done.

TERIYAKI FISH FILLET

Place a medium-sized fillet on an 18-by-18-inch piece of foil. Top the fillet with sliced green pepper and onion. In a small bowl, combine 2 tablespoons lemon juice, 1 tablespoon brown sugar and 1 tablespoon soy sauce (or a single restaurant packet). Pour the mixture over the fish and vegetables. Wrap and seal the foil. Cook for 15 to 20 minutes.

TIP CONTRIBUTORS

GENERAL-PURPOSE TIPS

Long Live the Leeches: Jim Keuten, owner, Jim's Bait, Duluth, MN. *No More Messy Worms:* Larry Bollig, Ham Lake, MN. *Bring the Worms to You:* Larry Ehardt, South Fork, CO. *Keep Crawlers Lively:* T.L. Hegeholz, Holcombe, WI. *Follow Birds to Fish:* Larry Bollig. *Acclimate Minnows:* Jim Keuten. *Finer Fiddle for Worms:* George Huber, Etlan, VA. *Sea Anchor Savvy:* Dave Diffely, Parshall, ND. *Heading off a Bird's Nest:* Bill Murphy, big-bass specialist, El Cajon, CA. *Cut a Backlash Short:* Timothy Maxey, Concord, VA. *Trigger Strikes While Trolling:* Rod Sather, fishing guide, Devils Lake, ND. *Bobber Helps You Get Unsnagged:* Ray Mertes, Trempealeau, WI. *Bonus for Paddlers:* John Herrick, owner, Moose Bay Co., Ely, MN. *More Accurate Spinning:* Steve Rajeff, tournament casting champion, Suquamish, WA. *No-Tangle Throw Rope:* David Marquardt, Forest Lake, MN. *Easy-to-See Ice-Fishing Line:* Bill Cork, Plano Molding Co., Plano, IL. *Comfort Is Important, Simplest Is Best, Any Fish Is a Prize:* Steve Grooms.

LARGEMOUTH & SMALLMOUTH BASS TIPS

Better "Pegging" Technique: Steve Lindberg, Woodbury, MN. *Mono Loop Fends off Weeds:* Larry Bollig. *Keep Curly-Tails From Twisting:* Skip Adams, tournament angler, Sebring, FL. *Plastic Surgery Improves Worms:* Ronnie Kovach; tournament angler, Huntington Beach, CA. *Wind in Rushes Triggers Bass:* Larry Bollig. *Secret Humps:* Mike Mladenik, fishing guide, Crivitz, WI. *Band Jigs for Bass:* Ronnie Kovach. *Write off Weeds:* Frankie Dusenka, owner, Frankie's Live Bait, Chisago City, MN. *Add Spice to Spinnerbaits:* Don Brauer, tournament angler, Fort Lauderdale, FL. *Vertical Jigging From a Distance:* Colin Stass, Blenheim, Ontario. *Prevent Line Twist With Bass Bugs:* Mark Emery, fishing guide, Oklawaha, FL. *Good Vibrations:* Woo Daves, professional angler, Chester, VA. *Looking for Active Fish:* Dick Garlock, professional angler, Alexandria Bay, NY. *Stick to Bread-and-Butter Spots:* Bill Murphy. *Finding Weedline Bass:* Kurt Johnson, tournament angler, Plymouth, MN. *Slow and Subtle:* Shaw E. Grigsby, Jr., professional angler, Gainesville, FL. *"Doodlin'" Brass and Glass:* Don Iovino, professional angler, Burbank, CA. *Jigging a Worm in Place:* Dick Garlock. *Target Shallow Weeds:* Kurt Johnson.

WALLEYE & SAUGER TIPS

A Rocky Start for Walleyes: Joe Bucher, fishing guide, Boulder Junction, WI. *Go Light After a Cold Front:* Tom Neustrom, Deer River, MN. *Double Bait for Big Fish:* Kent Oderman, Parshall, ND. *Jigs for Weed Walleyes:* Joe Bucher. *A Long Reach Means Fewer Snags, Slip in on Walleyes:* Jim Keuten. *Cure for Balled-up Leeches:* David H. Ohrtman, Chisaago City, MN. *Cut Through Stringy Weeds:* Tom Neustrom. *Improved Willow Rig:* Dick Grzywinski, fishing guide, St. Paul, MN.

NORTHERN PIKE & MUSKIE TIPS

Add Flash to Muskie Lures: Joe Bucher; Gene Curtis, Phelps, WI. *Muskies After Dark, Improve Glidebait Action, Weight Bucktails Quickly, Split Rings Improve Hooking, Protect Hands From Sharp Teeth:* Joe Bucher. *Bucktails With Spice:* George Sandell, Eden Prairie, MN. *More Hookups on Jerkbaits:* Mark Windels, owner, Windels Tackle Co., Crookston, MN. *Continuous Figure Eight:* Tom Gelb, Milwaukee, WI. *Finer Points of Figure-Eighting:* Joe Bucher; Don Pursch, fishing guide, Walker, MN; Paul Thorne Brothers Custom Rod & Tackle, Fridley, MN; Mark Windels. *Better Hook Sets With Big Bait:* Joe Bucher; John Kuhn, Kona, HI. *Prevent Bait Tangles:* Don Scott, Allegan, MI. *Keeping the Kinks Out:* Mark Windels.

TROUT & SALMON TIPS

Wormin' for Salmon: Mark Emery. *Peanuts Give Bait a Lift:* Don Pursch. *Easy-to-See Strike Indicators:* Al Troth, fishing guide, Dillon, MT. *Double-Duty Steelhead Plug:* John Crawford, fishing guide, Lewiston, ID. *Better Fly Floatant:* Al Troth. *Keep Reels Dry When Wading:* Jim Keuten. *Watching Hard-to-See Flies:* Tom Helgeson, owner, Bright Waters Fly Fishing, Minneapolis, MN. *Stopping a Strong Run:* Bob Nicholson, fishing guide, Baldwin, MI. *"Unmatch" the Hatch to Take Trout:* Craig Woods, Dorset, VT. *Dacron Backing Saves Fly Reels:* Jim Keuten. *Pretied Tippets Save Time:* Kevin D. Becker, Plymouth, MN. *Add Yarn to an Egg Loop, No Cling Guides for Drift Fishing, Offbeat Colors for Steelhead:* Jim Keuten. *Get a Grip on Salmon:* Bob Nicholson. *Follow Shifting Plumes:* Capt. John Olson, New Berlin, WI. *An Ant for All Seasons:* J. R. Humphrey, St. Paul, MN. *Cheap No-Slip Soles:* Shawn Perich, Grand Marais, MN.

PANFISH TIPS

Finesse Picky Perch: Larry Bollig. *Outwit Fussy Crappies:* Joe Bucher. *Detect Light-Biters:* Chuck Thompson, Mt. Prospect, IL. *A Little Leech Lasts Longer:* Dennis Hunt, St. Paul, MN. *Modify Jigs for Papermouths:* Eddie Slater, owner, Slater Jigs, Indianola, MS. *Pennants for Panfish:* Dick Gasaway, Littleton, CO. *Scout Ice-Fishing Spots in Summer:* Jon Poehler, Detroit Lakes, MN. *Read Depth Through Bad Ice:* Dave Genz, Spring Lake Park, MN. *See Light Bites in the Dark:* Dan Goihl, Melrose, MN; Jon Poehler. *Super-Tough Perch Bait:* Dick Grzywinski. *Preserve Perch Eyes:* Bill Hammer, Lake City, MN. *Light up Ice-Fishing Holes:* Dick Grzywinski. *Chum for Panfish:* Dave Genz, Jon Poehler.

CATFISH TIPS

Keep Baitfish on a Short Leash: Doug Stange, editor, "The In-Fisherman" magazine, Brainerd, MN. *Line Release for Bank Fishing:* Gary Clancy, Byron, MN. *Keep Chicken Liver on the Hook:* Gary Clancy; Joel Vance, Jefferson City, MO. *Longer-Lasting Scent:* Eduard L. Telders, Renton, WA. *Enhance Natural Odor:* Jim Schneider, New Ulm, MN. *Keep Clam Meat on the Hook:* Eduard L. Telders. *Junkyard Slip-Sinkers:* Jim Schneider. *Tough up Bait:* Jim McDonald, Royal, IA. *Cats Want Leeches - Dead or Alive:* Gary Clancy. *Lift Baits Above Snags:* John Sellers, fishing guide, Cross, SC. *Feel Your Way Around Snags:* Doug Stange. *Steelheading for Catfish:* Steve Payne, Post Falls, ID.

MAKING & MODIFYING LURES

An Improved Texas Rig, Spinning Worms for Bass: Mark Emery. Pliable Pegs: Don Iovino. *Mow Weeds With a Spinnerbait:* Hank Gibson, professional angler, Keswick, Ontario. *Tuning Spinner Blades, Two-Way Trailer:* Joe Bucher. *Snag-Resistant Snake Plugs, Fizzing for Fish:* Mark Emery. *Fixing the Weak Link:* Joe Bucher. Quick Paint Stirrer: T.L. Hegeholz. *Finding the Leak:* John Storm, Storm Manufacturing Co., Norman, OK. *High-Vis Dry Flies:* J. R. Humphrey. *Tooth-Proof Streamers:* Hugh Langevin, Minneapolis, MN.

TACKLE TIPS

Budget Line Stripper: Dale Odom, Pittsburgh, IL. *Tame Springy Mono:* Ronnie Kovach. *The Cat's-Paw Connection:* Charles Westby, fishing guide, Belize City, Belize. *Save Your Slip Bobber:* Tom Pfister, Duluth, MN. *Better Spring-Lock Bobber:* Michael D. Mills, Warren, OH. *Bobber Getter:* Tony Thompson, Pearl, MS. *Vest-Pocket Tackle Box:* Steve Murray, Clear Lake, IA. *Organize Your Worm Hooks:* Bruce Holt, G. Loomis Co., Woodland, WA. *Leader Tamer:* Robert Traczyk, Hurley, WI. *Straighten Up Snaps and Swivels:* Robert C. Hanna, Hillsdale, MI. *Controlling Leader Coils:* Capt. Butch LoSasso, Kona, HI. *Easy-Spinning Spinners:* Tom Neustrom. *Waterproofing Maps:* Cliff Jacobson, Hastings, MN. *Better Hook Sets With Diving Planes:* Bruce Holt. *Long-Distance Baitcasting:* Bob Ponds, Brandon. MS. *Keep Cold Metal Under Wraps:* Gene Schmidt, Shell Knob, MO. *Bundle Rods Quickly, No-Tangle Rods:* Bruce Holt. *Cane Pole Line Holder:* Steve Crawford, Eustis, FL. *Cork Caulk:* Gregg Thorne, Thorne Brothers Custom Rod & Tackle, Fridley, MN. *No-Slip Tiptop:* Bob Sonenstahl, Wayzata Bait & Tackle, Wayzata, MN. *Ultralong Ultralights:* Butch Furtman, host "Sportsman's Notebook," Duluth, MN. *Bank Fisherman's Strike Indicator:* Buck Baxter, Boise, ID; Ronnie Kovach. *Swivel Gaff:* George Collins, Charleston Heights, SC. *Replacing Rod Guides, Tying Multistrand Leaders:* Tom Neustrom. *A Better Needle Knot:* Mark Emery. *Manageable Marabou:* T.L. Hegeholz.

EQUIPMENT TIPS

Pinpoint Pinholes: Cliff Jacobson. *Personal Bug Deflectors:* Mark Emery. *Substitute Transducer Bracket:* Joe Bucher. *Understand Your Blind Spot:* Larry Bollig. *Get Better Readings Through the Ice:* Dave Genz. *Big "Hooks" Can Be Misleading, Avoid Depth Finder Interference:* Larry Bollig. *Portable Anchor:* Dan Makowsky, Duluth, MN. *Bargain Wading Staff:* J.R. Humphrey. *Snagproof Anchor:* Dan Makowsky, Duluth, MN. *Bargain Wading Staff:* J.R. Humphrey. *Cheaper Propane:* Jon Poehler. *Long-Lasting Trailer Lights:* Steve Crawford. *Don't Tire While Tubing:* Tom Anderson, The Fly Angler tackle shop, Fridley, MN. *Cold-Climate Boat Storage:* Greg Harvey, Grumman Boats, Marathon, NY.

TAKING CARE OF YOUR FISH

Mounting Preparation: Don Berger, Forest Lake, MN; Steve Crawford. *Quick and Easy Shore Lunches:* Billy Joe Cross, Mark Emery.

Creative Publishing international
is your Complete Source of How-to Information for the Outdoors

Available Outdoor Titles:

Hunting Books
- Advanced Turkey Hunting
- Advanced Whitetail Hunting
- Bowhunting Equipment & Skills
- The Complete Guide to Hunting
- Dog Training
- Elk Hunting
- How to Think Like a Survivor
- Hunting Record-Book Bucks
- Mule Deer Hunting
- Muzzleloading
- Outdoor Guide to Using Your GPS
- Pronghorn Hunting
- Whitetail Hunting
- Whitetail Techniques & Tactics
- Wild Turkey

Fishing Books
- Advanced Bass Fishing
- The Art of Freshwater Fishing
- The Complete Guide to Freshwater Fishing
- Fishing for Catfish
- Fishing Rivers & Streams
- Fishing Tips & Tricks
- Fishing with Artificial Lures
- Inshore Salt Water Fishing
- Kids Gone Fishin'
- Largemouth Bass
- Live Bait Fishing
- Modern Methods of Ice Fishing
- Northern Pike & Muskie
- Offshore Salt Water Fishing
- Panfish
- Salt Water Fishing Tactics

- Smallmouth Bass
- Striped Bass Fishing: Salt Water Strategies
- Successful Walleye Fishing
- Trout
- Ultralight Fishing

Fly Fishing Books
- The Art of Fly Tying
- The Art of Fly Tying – CD ROM
- Complete Photo Guide to Fly Fishing
- Complete Photo Guide to Fly Tying
- Fishing Dry Flies – Surface Presentations for Trout in Streams
- Fly-Fishing Equipment & Skills
- Fly Fishing for Beginners
- Fly Fishing for Trout in Streams
- Fly-Tying Techniques & Patterns

Cookbooks
- All-Time Favorite Game Bird Recipes
- America's Favorite Fish Recipes
- America's Favorite Wild Game Recipes
- Babe & Kris Winkelman's Great Fish & Game Recipes
- Backyard Grilling
- Cooking Wild in Kate's Camp
- Cooking Wild in Kate's Kitchen
- Dressing & Cooking Wild Game
- The New Cleaning & Cooking Fish
- Preparing Fish & Wild Game
- The Saltwater Cookbook
- Venison Cookery

To purchase these or other Creative Publishing international titles, contact your local bookseller, or visit our website at **www.creativepub.com**